I0621467

Imam Hussain (PBUH):
The Martyr of the Pioneer Culture of Mankind

'Allamah Muhammad Taqi Ja'fari

Translated by
Shahriar Fassih

Top Ten Award
International Network Inc.

2023

Published by: Top Ten Award International Network Inc.

Vancouver, BC **CANADA**
Email: Info@TopTenAward.Net
www.toptenaward.net

Ordering Information:
Quantity sales. Special discounts are available on quantity purchases by universities, schools, corporations, associations, and others. For details, contact the "Sales Department" at the above mentioned email address.

Imam Hussain (PBUH), 'Allamah Muhammad Taqi Ja'fari, 1st Edition.
ISBN: 978-1-990451-97-3   Paperback

In the Name of Allah,
the All-beneficent, the All-merciful

Table of Contents

Preface

Ever since I began my studies in theology, I wished to write a book about the character of Imam Hussain (PBUH). In fact, I would have given my whole life to have someone like Victor Hugo write about Imam Hussain (PBUH).

Muhammad Taqi Jafari

The ship of mankind's deliverance needs no sea to move on, for it sails on every teardrop shed for Hussain – a teardrop arising deep out of the heart, arousing the soul and presents itself to Allah.
Once again, we are discussing the day of and the night of Ashura. The night of Ashura was the great day of mankind and the day of Ashura was the immense divinity of all days. It is a pity that those who have written about and described Ashura have neglected its very essence – justice, and nothing but justice.

We must mournfully admit that the essence of Ashura has remained unexplored and unexplained ever since the evening of the first Ashura itself. And as time passed, the truth failed to shine miraculously along the path of the awakening of mankind as it should have.

The infiltration of ethnical perceptions and deviant beliefs which arise out of insufficient care alone have brought about great harm to this eternal event by causing changes in how it is seen. Thus, it is the immense responsibility of conscientious scholars to re-edit accounts of this bloody event and, through documented and meticulous research, achieve an accurate analysis and evaluation of the "true essence of Ashura."

In short, if we agree that the passing of time is one of the factors influencing the effect of thoughts on the souls of a culture, now that a year has gone by since this book was written, scholars should review it and make the necessary preparations in order to convey and depict what great scholars of religion see as essential in such books. This way religious knowledge can be enhanced, and it can become available to the masses who are devoted to the Holy Prophet's progeny and those great men of Allah.

As new phenomena emerge and novel issues arise, it becomes a necessity to edit and refine religious teachings. Therefore, it is essential that committed advocates of religion fulfill their responsibilities regarding this heritage of great works. They need to have in mind this important point – there is no doubt that those endowed with a "pioneer culture" have two significant duties: they must safeguard and protect it, and allow everyone to be exposed to it.

If the two significant measures mentioned above are not taken, "dependent cultures" as well as mixed and stagnant ones will be imposed upon us by others using various means and in different ways. It is of great importance to be prepared to provide explicit, definite answers to "questions" and "doubts" in order to protect and propagate a pioneer culture, for the majority of the harmful blows, abnormal retreats, and dangerous feelings of defeat and helplessness arise out of the biased doubts and unanswered questions posed... Thus, it is our duty to be meticulous, careful and protective.

The present book provides a different point of view. This book presents readers with discussions in which the author endeavors to prove, based on obvious proofs and clear deductions, that the Holy Prophet's progeny should never become victims of narrow-minded approaches; their elevated status is by no means to be subjected to degradation. In fact, the message enlightening books such as the present one try to convey is that devotees of the Holy Prophet and his progeny ought not to fall into narrow paths void of intellectual or religious benefits – paths which lead to passing consequences and, as a result, the feeling of devotion and commitment toward leadership and religion will be saturated within a superficial domain. Thus, man will see no need to deeply examine and delve into the ocean of true, original knowledge presented by prophets who have delivered Allah's revelations to us.

Although the written part of this book is not voluminous and does not cover a wide range of issues, considering the valuable truths provided in every statement, there is no doubt that these sections are to be regarded as the origin of a line of thought which, a few centuries after the event of Ashura, attempts to discover the "right-religious way" and present readers interested in religion with this right path.

With undeniably rich analyses, Muhammad Taqi Jafari has presented points and ideas no well-informed scholar of theology interested in understanding Shiite teachings regarding Islamic leadership will find redundant or irrelevant. Anyone who would like to attain knowledge about the Holy Prophet and his progeny and their true status and position in the context of religion without falling into deviations will need to take such thoughts and perceptions into consideration and be aware of their content.

In fact, Hussain (PBUH) can be regarded as the goldsmith of truth; he is the summit of which "epic" serves as a mere mountain foot. His eternal statement – "If you do not believe in religion, at least be free-minded!" – Is still persistently true even after almost fourteen centuries, and heads for not only eternity but also a high position in the most elevated thoughts of its era's thinkers. The *Imam* is once again asking mankind to be at least of a free mind if they are not of religious faith, may humanity dawn from the horizon of freedom.

The present book, which consists of two parts, presents a new approach toward Imam Hussain (PBUH) and his uprising; "life" has been reiterated rather than "tragedy", "human rights" have been regarded more significantly rather than "legend", "mankind" has been taken into more important consideration than "history", and "conscience" has replaced "epic" as a focal point. Although the late Allamah Jafari did not live long enough to complete his work on Imam Hussain (PBUH), he nonetheless succeeded in providing new insight into the matter. He invited anthropologists and men of wisdom and conscience human beings to consider more deeply the basic connection between Ashura and the truth as well as Imam Hussain (PBUH) and mankind. With his eloquent writing, Jafari has used the incomparable greatness in Imam Hussain (PBUH) to invite all human beings to rise so that the mystery of humanity can be deciphered.

> *O philosophers, legal scholars, economists, politicians, literary figures, artists, authorities on psychological fields, analysts of the history of mankind and pioneers of pioneer culture! In the midst of the winding paths the last two centuries have gone through – and have come to be famously known as superhighways of science and freedom, a certain being called "mankind" has been lost! There is no more room for delay. We must rise and attempt to find human beings. In order to do so, we must not forget the pioneers of Allah's enlightening religion and true upholders of moral ethics. We are now in the early fifteenth century Hijra and the twenty-first century A.D. is also just around the corner, and the distance between one who claims "I shall not force a guest who has chosen my house as a refuge to leave my house, for that will put his life in danger, even though such an action may make my own life face peril as well" and another who believes that "I am the end and everyone and everything else is the means!" is, in fact, the distance between humanity and anti-humanity. To see how true this claim is, it would suffice to compare the originality, firmness, and power human life had in the previous eras with the nihilistic, futile human life we witness today.*

As this reprint of this book called for a revision in the titles and headings of the speeches and sermons, we are happy to inform readers that the titles have been chosen, in order to provide an updated version of this book, from the main ideas presented by the late Allamah in each speech.

The Allamah Jafari Institute would like to express, on behalf of all of those involved in writing and mystic knowledge, its sincere appreciation for the late Dariush Shahin, who contributed to the compilation of this book before he passed away. We also feel obliged to thank Manouchehr Sadouqi Suha, Abdullah Nasri, Shahram Taqizadeh Ansari, Muhammad Reza Javadi, Sayyid Muhammad Ali Qaem Maqami (Al- Hussaini), Azra Jafari, Roya Azizi Mousavi and many others for the valuable contributions they made to the publication of this book.

Thus, we present this book to all seekers of truth and knowledge; may their thoughts and intellectual endeavors be ever-dynamic, and may Allah help them successfully accomplish their attempts to better know Hussain – the "son of the truth."

The Allamah Jafari Institute

Ali Jafari - July 2017

Book One

Introduction

"Hussain is indeed mankind's beacon of guidance and the ship of deliverance."

The Holy Prophet Muhammad (PBUH)

The ship of mankind's deliverance needs no sea to move on, for it sails on every teardrop shed for Hussain – a teardrop arising deep out of the heart, arousing the soul and presents itself to Allah.

An Immense Pledge and an Eternal Promise-keeping

O Hussain, descendent of the noblest of humans, the beloved of all Allah-loving souls and the hope of all chaste children of Adam! Your bloody story took place in the scorching plains of Nainawa, centuries before our generation. That is why we, and a group of travelers in this meaningful passageway known as life, have been deprived of the chance to see your divinely glorious face and also your exceptional companions due to chronological differences.

Indeed, having brought about flourish in the most prosperous and the greatest virtues in their souls, your companions found wings deep within their hearts to fly from the narrow worldly realm high up to the world of purity. If only we had also found the chance to selflessly lose our lives for your sake on that bloody day, as did the seventy-two pure human beings accompanying you.

Nevertheless, we endlessly thank Allah that we were not among those unwise people who made pledges to you and invited you to their homeland of Iraq in order to uphold the state of righteousness and justice, for when you set foot onto their land, they broke their promises and wrote hundreds of letters of denial. Then, they attacked you and your men with their swords. Before the sun had set that day, they had the people of the world deprived of the shining sun of your existence. Little did they know that if the eternal beauty of your physical being fades away from the visible aspect of the world, it will, in fact, arise within the pure, chaste hearts of Adam's honest descendants in an even more profound manner.

Now, we devotees of your dear being, hereby have written a pledge with the pen of our reason, ration and conscience and signed it with our heart and our blood that we will love you and defend the divine mission you undertook – which is, in fact, the immense mission of mankind itself – until the last day of our lives. May we rise once again on Judgment Day seeing you and head toward our final destiny guided by the immense attraction of your soul.

Muhammad Taqi Jafari

June 11,1994

Part 1

Allah's Supreme Wisdom Allah's Wisdom Is Superior to Man's Limited Senses and Ration

It is Allah's immense wisdom which makes the human soul arise out of lifeless material – and, in the later stages, a few drops of sperm – and guides it way up to the highest degrees of beauty and perfection.

Moreover, it is Allah's divine wisdom which makes the most constructive of consequences occur after the most wicked events. Satan – due to the arrogance and pride he felt about his own origin, which consisted of fire – refused to prostrate before Adam (PBUH), thus disobeying Allah's command. As a result, Satan is degraded to the lowest of wicked states and is expelled out of Allah's court. Nonetheless, Satan is in position to deceive Adam's descendants, which allows them to achieve the highest levels of perfection due to the hardships and austerities they go through in order to disagree with and resist Satan's seductions.

It is due to Allah's immense wisdom that He has made the cruelest and most shameless crimes and brutalities committed by Yazid upon Hussain and Hussain's companions lead to the revival of Islam, humanity and its profound virtues.

We must note that Satan, in free will, refused to prostrate to Adam (PBUH). There are three reasons why Satan did so freely and voluntarily:

a. Allah had made Satan required to prostrate, and we know that being assigned to duty or responsibility without free will is obscene; it would be impossible for Allah to do so.

b. Allah then intensely scolded Satan for refusing to prostrate before Adam (PBUH).

c. Allah has set punishment for Satan, both in this world and in the afterworld.

Thus, people who are deceived by Satan's deceptions commit, in fact, sins and disobediences on their own free will. There are two reasons for this:

a. If Satan's deceptions compelled them to commits such acts, Allah would not be able to hold them liable for any responsibilities or duties.

b. As stated in the Holy Quran, Satan will claim on Judgment Day that:

> *Then reproach not me, but reproach your own souls. [I did not compel you to do such things, I merely seduced you and deceived you. You*

were equipped with reason and ration and intelligence, and were also
blessed with the teachings provided by the prophets.][1]

Moreover, the obnoxious act of crime committed by Yazid and his men arose out of their free will; no fatalistic factor compelled them to do something so shameful. If a wall fatalistically caves in on a few people and kills them, people would never condemn or damn that wall, while every conscious, dignified, honorable human being, when informed of the catastrophic crime committed by Yazid, intensely condemns and damns him for what he did. On the other hand, which natural, mental, even conventional factor led to such a horrific crime?! If we were to justify what Yazid did base on selfishness, passion for desires and lusts, greed for power and dominance and other factors such as worldly wishes and pleasures acting as fatalistic, compulsory factors, would there be a single criminal left throughout history?!

Thus, Yazid ibn Mu'awiyah acted out of free will and committed the most wicked sin of all – he killed Imam Hussain (PBUH) in such a cruel and catastrophic fashion that is unprecedented in history. In fact, this event has brought about a highly important result for Islamic communities: the glorious policy Imam Hussain (PBUH) used in order to uphold and revive Islam and human virtues is associated with his martyrdom and will be regarded as a pattern for human conduct as long as mankind exists. This excruciatingly painful incident, which provides mankind with the sacrifice of Hussain ibn Ali (PBUH) as an attempt to defend human greatness, dignity and honor, is an event great enough alone to save the history of humanity from suffering from oppression, atrocity and injustice as long as people's minds are sedated and washed cleaned of all righteousness-seeking and realism by the Yazids of the times.

Imam Hussain (PBUH): The Martyr of Mankind's Pioneer Culture

We offer our endless gratitude and appreciation to Allah Whose immense greatness, kindness, and divine wisdom led to the creation of meaningful human beings within a meaningful universe. Allah made man progress along the path of *"We are from Allah, and we shall eventually return to Allah as well,"* and in order to help man develop his character, Allah has provided him with two kinds of guides along this immense journey:

1. Man's internal guides – his soul, his ration and his innate nature, and
2. External guides, who are in fact Allah-sent prophets.

We send our endless gratitude and respect to the pure souls of all prophets, Imams and their sincere followers, for they rose and used all of their power and talents to guide human beings. Many of them even sacrificed themselves along this great path to save human lives from the contamination of material affairs and guide human beings toward the supreme goal of intelligible life.

A forerunner among these pioneers building up humanity is Imam

---

[1] The Holy Quran (Abraham 14:22).

Hussain (PBUH), who – considering all of the aspects and events regarding his martyrdom – stood tall and firm on the summit of selflessness and sacrifice for righteousness and the truth and cried out, clearly for all to hear:

> O human beings! There is a more elevated meaning to life, and that involves being located within the rays of the attraction of divine perfection. And for death, there is also a greater truth – entering the domain of the attraction of divine perfection.

The life depicted in the Imam's words is intelligible life, in which freedom, dignity, honor, knowledge, justice, honesty, sincerity, and seeking perfection are regarded as major components. Moreover, death in such a concept is the flourish of intelligible life, as the human character achieves its eternal end and purpose within the domain of the attraction of divine perfection. Indeed, this is true life, starting from Allah and culminating in Allah as well.

The Purpose for Writing This Book

I was born in and have lived in countries[2] where, over the years and on various occasions, in particular during the month of Muharram when people mourn for Imam Hussain (PBUH), the murmurs, weeping and cries for Imam Hussain (PBUH) have always been hears and have redrawn everyone's attention toward the immensity of human values and principles – which Imam Hussain (PBUH) heroically rose to defend. As a young adult, while listening to rich speeches made by learned authorities who spoke sincerely about the history of early Islam, particularly the unique event which occurred in the plain of Nainawa, I grew quite curious about this amazing event. Then, as I gradually became more familiar with the Turkish, Persian and Arabic literature describing the incomparable event of Karbala [and the conflict it involved between two majorly opposing parties], I grew more and more attracted to and interested in the subject.

Throughout the years I was a student, whether, in Iran or Najaf, I always spent some of the time studying this amazing event in the history of mankind as well as its causes and consequences. As I was engaged in such internal thoughts and influences, I also saw countless people – young or old, commoners or great thinkers and distinguished figures and authorities – shed the sincerest, heartfelt tears when reminded of the bloody event of Karbala; indeed, they wept even more sorrowfully than they would for the loss of their dearest ones. These sacred tears arising out of pure hearts and pouring out righteousness-loving eyes can alone protect the principles of human virtue and greatness forever. Such sacred, chaste tears [which are indicative of the pure life led by the weepers] originate from Hussain's pureblood as well as the pure blood of his companions shed upon the scorching plain of Nainawa. Naturally, as long as this divine source continues flowing within

---

[2] Iran, and the fairly long period of time I spent in Najaf, where most of my studies took place.

pure human souls, tears shed for Hussain (PBUH) will also keep flowing.

These continual mental states and spiritual waves I experienced throughout the years gave me a very special feeling; as a result, I felt the great desire to – Allah-willing, and to the best of my capability – present an analysis and interpretation of the unique event of Karbala and examine and evaluate as carefully as possible the reasons and consequences of this great event (which indeed is totally unprecedented and uncontested throughout the world) to all supporters of human dignity and all victims of the highest of human virtues.

If thinkers and authorities of the humanities considered the story of this event – which presents quite well the eternity of mankind's mission – from the point of view presented using the interpretation and analysis in this book, they would undoubtedly reconsider what the true definition of "mankind" should be. Moreover, they would certainly also admit the fact that as mankind cannot be fully known without having explored and discovered man's natural, mental and psychological talents and potentials first, the merit-based truths about human beings cannot be explored unless mankind's highly varied spiritual talents and potentials are discovered, either. Thus, it is hoped that they may shift their approach toward exploring and discovering mankind, and instead of focusing on human behavior – which is merely an appearance of a limited range of the aspects concerned with humanity – they should achieve a true knowledge of human beings and their various potentials and capabilities. If thinkers of the humanities or philosophy are not aware that the human beings they are attempting to discover can reach a pinnacle of perfection in character such as Hussain (PBUH) and, on the other hand, can reach lowly levels of degradation and decadence such as Yazid, they had better avoid making any remarks about the nature or characteristics of mankind at all.

As years went by, not only did this great desire fail to wane inside me, but in fact, the more I delved into mental activities and intellectual endeavors in the humanities and witnessed its insolvable problems and issues [indeed, there is no way to interpret and resolve these problems except turn to and acknowledge the truths about human virtues and values], the greater the desire grew. On the other hand, the years went by at amazing speed, and as the future kept becoming part of the past, I was continually busy making work sense of duty obliged me to. Then, early in the fifteenth century Hijra (i.e., in the late twentieth century A.D.), the fresh breezes of life faded away, and evil cries of futility and aimlessness in life took their place everywhere – the disease of "self-alienation" had broken out. I saw it necessary to rush to the aid of those who endeavored to wake the self-alienated, intoxicated human beings of our era. I hope this may serve and promote the advancement of the divine immensity of life and its elevated goal, and help people realize how decadent and degraded "lowly" death – i.e., the demise of human virtues – can be.

Writing this book began in the Muharram of 1415 Hijra. I decided to entitle the book "Imam Hussain (PBUH): The Martyr of the Pioneer Culture of Mankind." The term "culture" implies quite rich content, particularly when specified to "pioneer" and "mankind," for the pioneer culture of mankind would mean:

The way of intelligible life in the attraction field of divine perfection based on evolutionary principles and values which all prophets of Allah and great men of wisdom have devoted themselves – and some have even sacrificed themselves in the process – to interpret, propagate and preach. There is no doubt that Ali ibn Abi Talib's dear son, Hussain Ibn Ali (PBUH) – the hero of how a life of dignity and honor is to be manifested and interpreted – is among the first and foremost of such great men when it comes to endeavors for the sake of humanity. The shining blood of this interpreter of life, the great man who proved what the aim of human beings' existence in this world is, can be regarded as the second sign for the eternity of mankind and the mission mankind has been given.

As the Arab writer, poet and philosopher Abul Ala Al-Ma'arri have described it, such signs are revealed at the beginning of and also at the end of every day:

> There are two things upon the forehead of time which serve as witnesses to the blood of two martyrs [Ali (PBUH) and his son Hussain (PBUH)]:
> the first comes at the end of the night and the start of the day [the blood which flowed from the head of Ali ibn Abi Talib (PBUH)],
> and the second occurs at the bloody sunset every day when night falls [the blood of Hussain (PBUH)].
> These two great witnesses are a fixed part of every day in time, and on Judgment Day, they will be in Allah's Court in order to present their complaint to Allah.

Before setting about the main contents this book intends to discuss, we shall go through ten introductions needed in order to analyze and interpret a major event like this:

1. The first introduction involves three fundamental ways to save man from vanity and prove and manifest the divine greatness of life (intelligible life).

2. The second introduction states that accurate knowledge and judgment regarding any major event in history arising to uphold and arouse values depends upon three important factors.

3. The third introduction presents examples of two different approaches toward historical events.

4. The fourth introduction discusses the fact that human life will, in fact, be the lowliest and degraded phenomenon in all of the nature unless it is recognized accurately and its supreme goal is not fully explained.

5. The fifth introduction explores human life and its inherent greatness

and dignity as seen in Islamic human rights.

6. The sixth introduction poses a question: Islam has set defending the honor and dignity of life as one of its basic principles, and life has been the purpose of the amazing event in Nainawa, but what is life?

7. The seventh introduction is a discussion on the five principles of power, righteousness, and evil.

8. The eighth introduction involves the two basic pillars of characters who build the pioneer culture of humanity – both of which Imam Hussain (PBUH) has in their highest form.

9. The ninth introduction pertains to the most fundamental factor leading to the occurrence of this amazing event: the profound faith and love Imam Hussain (PBUH) had for Islam, the most logical, and the clearest of human religions, the religion in which defending human life and its honor and divine dignity is seen as one of the most important principles.

10. The tenth introduction discusses what is expected of scholars of the humanities as sees by various sects of Islam in the first place and then other thinkers of divine and human religions regarding careful attention to the unique sacrifice made by Imam Hussain (PBUH) to save human values.

It is recommended that dear readers study the introductions mentioned above having gained some familiarity with the contents of this book, for they depict the scientific and philosophical aspects of the research this book intends to achieve.

Part 2

**The First Introduction: Three Fundamental Ways to Save
Man from Vanity and Prove and Manifest the Divine
Greatness of Life (Intelligible Life)**

In order to fulfill the vital service of proving and stating the divine greatness
of life and its supreme goal, there are three ways, and the necessity to
present them through the observation of the truth about life and pure
internal intuition have been reiterated and depicted by history, man's pure
conscience and, most important of all, Allah.

1. The divine instructions presented by Allah's great prophets and true
   men of wisdom and those who have released themselves from the
   darknesses of material affairs and joined the elevated realm of ration
   and reason need to be presented logically. Theologians and chaste
   scholars of profound thought have made the sincerest and diligent
   efforts to propagate these teachings, and are still persevering with
   their endeavors.
2. The constructive and positive results of following Allah-sent
   religions and human beings trained by Allah's prophets and people
   who have purified themselves of all contaminations, selfishnesses,
   and despotism must be collected and studied. It is obvious that
   Allah-sent religions have made the most significant contribution
   toward the purification of human souls and the refinement of moral
   ethics and making mankind familiar with the supreme goal of life
   throughout history, thus having an important role in the progress of
   pioneer culture. This is plain truth, even though most contemporary
   Western historians and sociologists [who see man's evolutionary
   progress as terminating in the unconscious, fatalistic movements of
   the "machine"] have shown no tendency toward making a study of,
   admitting to, or presenting people with this vital role of Allah-sent
   religions so that the machinery-stricken communities of our times
   may use.

Some may object and say that if Allah-sent religions truly could make
a constructive contribution to the evolution of mankind, historians would
never conceal that. The answer is quite simple: unfortunately, most
historians regard their duty as merely collecting the effects of events in
history from their own certain point of view rather than providing analyses

or interpretations. These historians, as well as sociologists, are content to just know about phenomena and the consequences of various behaviors displayed by people; they pay no attention to the causes and reasons for human behaviors and potentials!

Those who conceal such reasons and highly important human potentials can be categorized into two main groups:

    a.   Those who do not regard themselves as capable of understanding such reasons; therefore, seeing no talent or potential for doing so within themselves, they did not attempt to examine such reasons, and sometimes even deny them.

    b.   As Max Planck, the renowned German physicist has stated:

> It is no accident that all great thinkers of all eras of history have been so profoundly religious, even though they may have never expressed or displayed such beliefs.[3]

Of course, the reason or reasons behind this lack of revealing of such beliefs calls for further research so that we may find out why they decide to keep their religious tendencies unknown to others.

    3.   The third way, which is of high importance, involves the profound love and enthusiasm pure-hearted, wise human beings have for being blessed with supreme spiritual greatness and merits, even though it may be tedious, difficult and even painful to obtain them. Having found themselves within the field of divine attraction (i.e., the tendency to find Allah), the extreme limit of such virtues and dignities is various kinds of sacrifices and martyrdoms in order to protect oneself or others from physical or spiritual poverty. If human life did not have a goal superior to worldly desires and earthly benefits, not only would all of such virtues, sacrifices, acts of honor and martyrdoms prove futile and in vain, but also those human beings of fine virtues who had gone through a great deal of suffering and hardship in order to achieve such virtues and had even lost their natural life for this purpose would have to be regarded as helpless, weak and even pitiful people[4], for instead of making the most of the worldly pleasures and fulfilling their personal desires, they decided to avoid all of the benefits and joys in life and tolerate many painful hardships and disturbances. Some even lost the dearest thing of all – their very own sweet lives!

We must speak explicitly and have no fear of the anti-human statements

---

[3] Planck, Max (1932): *Where Is Science Going?*

[4] Centuries ago, Naser Khusrow Qubadiani, the renowned Iranian poet, stated why this is so:

Time and the universe would be just a plaything

if the long day of this world were to have no tomorrow...

made by men like Thomas Hobbes[5] or Nietzsche.[6] If Genghis Khans in Asia and Nero in Europe failed to deliver the final, fatal blow to humanity with all of the killings and bloodshed they created, people like the diseased ones mentioned above, consciously or unconsciously, will. They will bring about the demise of humanity because what they say will make cultures and civilizations to deteriorate and human emotions and the finest and most divine of human feelings to be destroyed – which is why the conference in Vancouver, Canada[7] was concerned whether mankind would, in fact, live to see the twenty-first century or not. The reason why they will eventually bring about the end of all of the humanity is that the corruption of moral ethics, the deterioration of civilizations and cultures, and the outbreak of hedonism will guide life toward futility; thus, people will have no hearts or souls left to be able to get a taste of true life.

To further explain the third way, we shall briefly discuss the meaning of martyrdom. Unfortunately, most contemporary thinkers of the humanities, particularly in the West, have failed to devote enough attention to the significance of the divine phenomenon of martyrdom.

The phenomenon of martyrdom is so highly significant that even if there were only one martyr during the whole history of mankind, it would be sufficient to prove the fine rhythm of the universe – which depicts the supreme goal of life. However, there have been dozens of, maybe even hundreds of, thousands of martyrs throughout history, those who, having

---

[5] Thomas Hobbes (1588-1679) was an English philosopher. An extreme materialist, he saw the society as a machine which can only be operated by the power of its engineer or leader. He stated that human beings differed in their main nature, and all human beings are savage and criminal. Hobbes believed that a leader or a king needs to have unlimited power – in a word, a leader must be tyrannical and despotic. He regarded human beings as wolves. (See Thomas, Henry, & Thomas, Dana Lee (1941): *Living Biographies of Great Philosophers.*) [Translator]

[6] Friedrich Wilhelm Nietzsche (1844-1900) was a German philosopher, cultural critic, poet, and Latin and Greek scholar whose work has exerted a profound influence on Western philosophy and modern intellectual history. Some of his beliefs can be summed up as: a) Be dangerous, and live as if you are at war. b) To be a creator, one must be a destroyer first and wipe out all ancient values and virtues. c) The ancient gods are dead; there are no gods left. Now there are only supermen. d) For a superman, there are only moral principles for classes rather than moral principles for the masses; in other words, the masses are at the service of the classes. e) A group of people need to be destroyed in order to make a superman. (See ibid.) [Translator]

[7] From September 10 to 15, 1989, a symposium was held in Vancouver, Canada, in which about 20 scientists from all over the world took part. The topic on the agenda at the symposium was "Survival in the 21st Century". In this symposium, people of various societies around the world were asked to take collaborate, collective measures so that the twenty-first century would not prove to be mankind's last. (See Jafari, Muhammad Taqi, *Universal Human Rights.*)

elevated and perfected their personalities, gave up their natural life in order to achieve true life and defend humanity and its values and virtues.

We shall now set about a concise study of the phenomenon of martyrdom. The following explanations are, in fact, but a brief description of some aspects of this immense truth.

What Is Martyrdom?

Martyrdom means putting an end to the flow of life [which is the absolute desirable thing in the context of nature] in full awareness and familiarity with the nature and specifications of life and with the orientation which we shall now discuss.

Some Aspects of Martyrdom

1. Putting an end to one's life in order to defend the values, virtues and real lives of the members of the community.
2. Freeing oneself of one's physical embodiment and allowing the human spirit to fly up to achieve the level of divine intuition and the attraction of perfection as an effort to appreciate one's own intelligible life as well as those of others.
3. Determining the criterion for a justifiable life in this world.

Of course, it is obvious that those who are inconsiderate toward the truth and real value of life and regard life as merely eating, sleeping and fulfilling their animal desires are capable of comprehending neither martyrdom nor true life – which is of the highest merit and value of all.

In order to take into consideration how immensely significant martyrdom is, it is essential to understand two truths:

1. The absolute importance of life; and
2. The importance of the goal martyrdom intends to achieve.

It is by understanding the two truths above that we can comprehend what it means to lose one's life voluntarily and with utmost awareness and delight.

A great deal has been said about the incredible significance and immensity of life. Here we shall just confine our discussion to one point. Let us say a human being is enjoying the immense blessing of life – i.e., a person of completely balanced physical and mental well-being – is given a choice:

1. To continue life and be endowed with reason, intellect, conscience and other potentials for perfection, or
2. Own the whole universe while undergoing disturbances and disorders in life and its immensity and benefits.

A conscious human being of sound sense and mental stability will obviously choose to continue a life of physical and mental health.

The more aware the martyred human being is of the benefits and immensities of life, and the more capable the martyred human being is when it comes to using them, the greater and more valuable his martyrdom will be.

Examples of the Greatness of Human Life

When humans are alive, they:

- enjoy beauty,
- use their reason, ration, and conscience,
- show affection and love,
- make explorations,
- intuitively discover truths,
- acknowledge the immense elegance of the universe,
- defend justice and righteousness,
- appreciate intelligible freedom and free will,
- are enlightened by knowledge and ideology,
- enjoy serving their fellow humans,
- are capable of bringing about civility and prosperity in the world,
- acknowledge the satisfaction brought about by lawfulness and orderliness,
- are overjoyed by bringing about a revival in their fellow humans,
- understand emotions and connections,
- discover and explore the immensity of their internal feelings by means of making artistic innovations,
- save their fellow human beings and provide the grounds for their evolutionary progress through healthy rational and mental endeavors,
- Discover the universe within their own selves as they widen and develop the dominance of their own "selves" upon the universe.

It is obvious that the advantages and immensities in life are countless. A conscious, aware human being will, in fact, lose a whole world by losing each of these advantages or immensities, for each of them alone can serve as the aim of and justify one's life. Now we can well understand why Imam Hussain's martyrdom is the greatest martyrdom ever to emerge in the history of mankind; despite knowing about all of the aspects and advantages of life and being endowed with them, he chose to lose a life.

Part 3

The Second Introduction: Accurate Knowledge and Judgment regarding Any Major Event in History Which Arose Aiming to Uphold Values Depends upon Three Important Factors

Factor 1: Obtaining as Much Sufficient, Necessary Information as We Can about Nature, Reasons, and Results of the Event

Factor 2: Obtaining as Much Awareness as Possible of the General, Fixed Principles, and the Partial, Variable Propositions

Factor 3: Having the Ability to Perceive the Real Taste of Supreme Human Principles and Virtues

Factor 1: Obtaining as Much Sufficient, Necessary Information as We Can about Nature, Reasons, and Results of the Event

Obviously, even the slightest and most unimportant events in one's individual or social life cannot be understood unless all of the reasons and causes influencing the event as well as other events occurring simultaneously are also examined and taken into account, let alone those major global historical events[8] which leave a profound impact on the physical and spiritual fate of all of the mankind. There is no doubt that the events regarding Imam Hussain (PBUH) provide a comprehensive and unique manifestation of every aspect of sacrifice for the greatest of human virtues. As stated quite explicitly in *Imam Hussain and Iran*, a book authored by a German researcher:

> *Hussain's being killed was [as is anyone's being killed] a disaster;*
> *however, it was an exceptional disaster, and fourteen centuries*
> *later, a neutral historian sees this disaster as a very high mountain,*
> *compared to which the disasters of other wars are totally outweighed*
> *and negligible. Perhaps the greatest reason for the greatness of this*
> *disaster is the fact that it did not occur in order to defend one's*
> *life, and there was no material incentive, either. Hussain was not*

---

[8] By calling the story of Karbala "global", we mean that the truths and realities observed in the series of causes and values regarding this event are not confined to only one specific land, ethnic race or culture, for this event pertains to human beings, and can be considered as the most vivid example of conflict between two opposing groups: 1. advocates of absolute righteousness and 2. advocates of absolute evil.

interested in becoming a lasting name by sacrificing himself. In fact,
it was others who made his name linger on and be remembered.[9]

An important question arises here. Given the immense significance, the story of this event has, particularly regarding its causes and its consequences, why have most researchers and analysts of general history – despite having made studies of the event – failed to deal with it with deserving reverence and sufficient attention? There seem to be four main reasons behind the lack of attention paid to this important event:

1.   In order to study this incredible event thoroughly, one needs to discover and fully know a large variety of aspects and levels such as knowledge of religion, ethics, law, and politics – in other words, knowledge of how human beings should be managed and guided toward the highest goal of life and the principles of pioneer cultures. That is why few people have managed to fully comprehend the true significance of this event.

2.   To comprehend an event which is being analyzed, sometimes it is necessary to study the reasons and factors – whether major or minor – as well as the consequences and other concurrent events which may pertain to the incident studied. If analysts fail to gather all of such details, they will be unable to accurately comprehend the event.

3.   If the comprehensive knowledge of the event makes the researcher abandon some of his personal beliefs, he will certainly have no interest in gaining complete knowledge of the event.

Given the reasons mentioned above, we can see why most authors and historians have been unable to achieve an accurate, meticulous treatise of this incredible, constructive event in history.

In this case, we should take into consideration Mr. Kurt Frischler, the German researcher and author of *Imam Hussain and Iran*. Despite the extensive study he has presented and the highly useful ideas he has implied regarding Imam Hussain's story, Frischler has studied the event completely separate from its roots and previous events. In fact, if one has no information about the events which occurred before the year 61 after Hijra, one would presume that the amazing tale of Nainawa took place in a period of history before which no event had occurred at all!

Furthermore, in another part of the book mentioned above, Imam Hussain (PBUH) has been reported to have said to Al-Farazdaq:[10]

For years, I just waited and did not attempt to fight the fundamentals
of oppression and announce what was righteous; but now, after a

---

[9] Frischler, Kurt (1977): *Imam Hussain and Iran.*

[10] Hammam ibn Ghalib (born c. 641; died 728–730), most commonly known as Al-Farazdaq or Abu Firas, was an Arabian poet. [Translator]

long hiatus of silence, I have decided to rise to the challenge.[11]

What history tells us, however, is:

> *When Imam Hassan (PBUH) passed away, a movement was started by the Shiites of Iraq. In a letter to Imam Hussain (PBUH), they claimed that they had broken off their allegiance to Mu'awiyah, and will shift their allegiance to Imam Hussain (PBUH) instead. Imam Hussain disagreed, however; he reminded them that he was under obligation due to an arrangement he had with Mu'awiyah. He was unable to violate that agreement for a certain period of time. Nonetheless, in the case of Mu'awiyah's death, he would consider their suggestion.*

We see that Imam Hussain (PBUH) did not sit idly regarding oppression; when the chance to fight tyranny and wrongdoing came up, his response was not to merely remain silent. The plentiful, highly powerful reasons we have to lead us to the conclusion that Imam Hussain (PBUH) never, in fact, turned his back to the principle of *Ihda-al-Husnayain*;[12] he had no problem with being killed for Allah. Therefore, the following quotation does not seem to be accurate:

> *Abu Herreh Azdi saw Imam Hussain heading for Kufa. 'O son of the Prophet of Allah! Why did you leave Allah's sacred home?' 'O Abu Herreh,' Imam Hussain (PBUH) replied, 'The Bani-Umayyads took my property from me, but I remained patient. They insulted me, but I took it. They wanted to kill me, but I saved myself. And I swear to Allah that a group of tyrants will kill me, and Allah will immerse them into humiliation, degradation, and sharp swords; Allah will have someone who will humiliate them dominate over them, a humiliation even worse than the people of Sheba ...*[13]

Even if it were accurate, first of all, Imam Hussain (PBUH) was patient and prudent when it came to personal issues – as Imam Hassan Mujtaba (PBUH) had been – rather than remaining silent in the face of oppression toward all Islamic societies. Secondly, given the commitment the Imam had toward Mu'awiyah due to the agreement they had, his toleration and patience regarding the injustices and violations Imam Hussain (PBUH) personally underwent did not mean he would be allowed to start a battle against Mu'awiyah. (It should be noted, however, that according to the book *Luhuf*, the above statements of Imam Hussain's were addressed to Abu-Herreh rather than Al-Farazdaq.)

    4.   The fourth reason, which may be the most important one, is that

---

[11] Frischler, Kurt (1977): *Imam Hussain and Iran.*

[12] This principle presents two ways – one should either live a life of dignity and honor or die an honorable death trying to achieve the supreme goal of life.

[13] Sayyid ibn Tawus, *Luhuf ("Sighs of Sorrow").*

when studying the Karbala event, researchers and thinkers are concerned with truths such as faith, love, an immense sense of duty regarding all human beings and a powerful belief in Allah and eternity. One of the parties involved – Imam Hussain (PBUH) and his men – were endowed with these truths as hugely as one could be endowed. However, the other party – Yazid and his men – knew no logic other than selfishness, tyranny, and oppression. No matter how hard a researcher may try to take an impartial, unaffected stance toward the two logics mentioned above (i.e., absolute righteousness and absolute evil), it will be impossible for him to remain uninfluenced. Indeed, it is the great influence of the tale of Nainawa that has, throughout history, made individuals, as well as societies, start progressing toward evolutionary goals. With some careful attention, we will see the noticeable impact Imam Hussain's movement has had when it comes to human virtues and values. When studying this event – which involves the confrontation of humanity with inhumanity – researchers can see the two extremes of greatness and perfection on one hand and degradation and evil on the other with utmost vividness and clarity; no reasonable researcher or logical thinker truly familiar with mankind would possibly fail to be affected by Imam Hussain's supernatural attraction. We are all aware that if one is attracted by such a great character, all animal-like qualities, greed for power, domineering features, selfishness and lust for fame will fade away. How few, nevertheless, are those who will give up these things to achieve that attraction.

Indeed, this is how human beings can be degraded down to the lowest of immoral evils. These people are like mice digging away and making holes under the earth and beneath walls. Even when they come to light, they will run away and keep on digging away in the dark!

Factor 2: Obtaining as Much Awareness as Possible of the General, Fixed Principles, and the Partial, Variable Propositions

To understand how significant this factor is, we should first take into consideration two fundamental aspects about historical events:

The First Aspect: The Partial, Variable Effects and Currents of Events

This aspect is concerned with the sequence of historical events in connection with the physical causes and effects as well as simultaneous events. As seen from this aspect, history is a combination of physical, variable, partial appearances which we witness more or less for a while as variable, partial, observable parts of time and use them by means of our intellect, reason and the tools we have. It is due to this continual, partial quality that the study of the effects and appearances of physical events in history has not yet been regarded as a science.

The Second Aspect: Without Paying Careful Attention to the General, Fixed Principles, and Laws about Events in History, It Would Be Impossible to Interpret, Justify or Compare Such Events

These laws and principles can be categorized into two main groups:

The First Group: First-degree Principles and Laws based on Vastness and Comprehensiveness, such as the motivation factor of history and the main fundamentals of the principles of the humanities – for instance, the fixed, general rules of law, economics, politics and moral ethics. It is a fixed, general principle, for example, that "the motive factor of history consists of 1. any truth beneficial for humans and 2. humans' managing of their own lives"; this principle can explain the various aspects pertaining the fundamentals underlying historical events and movements. Moreover, the main basis of law in history, for instance, states that since every human being has unlimited tendencies and wishes and social life would be impossible if all of the mankind were to fulfill their endless tendencies, human beings need to eliminate those tendencies of theirs which lead to disturbance, inconvenience, and killing and accept limited wishes which could make life in the society possible.

The Second Group: Secondary Principles and Laws; this group involves the principle of dividing beneficial truths into physical and spiritual ones and also dividing the principles emerging from the analysis of each of these general truths, such as rules concerning agriculture, moral ethics as well as political and legal principles.

Factor 3: Having the Ability to Perceive the Real Taste of Supreme Human Principles and Virtues

For those who sport a superficial approach and see human beings and their history as merely a complex animal along with natural effects and consequences along with a continuous sequence called "history," this factor is not only regarded as insignificant but not even worthy of consideration for historians. As Kurt Frischler has quoted from Marquardt in his book *Imam Hussain and Iran*:

> *If a historian becomes interested in a person mentioned in history, he is, in fact, one of the faithful rather than a historian.*

To analyze the theory mentioned above, if Marquardt meant to imply a historian's allowing his faith in an individual involved in an event influence the features and factors concerned with the story, such an approach is wrong, and Marquardt himself has also stated so. When an event occurs in the universe, it is the event itself that has emerged due to certain reasons in history rather than the tendencies and beliefs of the historian per se. If Marquardt is conveying that research upon historical events should include no evaluation or judgment, such an idea will prove unacceptable; if thinkers engaged in the study of the history of mankind were mere to narrate events one after another and present them to their contemporaries and the next generations, and if those who read about these events make no assessment or judgment about what should have happened, we would in fact be removing the most fundamental sources of the principles and laws of human beings' intelligible life as well as its values and anti-values from the viewpoint of the humanities. Thus, the philosophy of history, analyzing history and drawing conclusions from history would be confined to watching a series of lifeless events which seem like random occurrences. By encouraging historians to be absolutely neutral and impartial regarding historical events, particularly events which can influence mankind, we would, in fact, be eliminating principles and fundamentals from the humanities and leaving nothing but physical, animal-like knowledge!

Of course, it is quite unlikely that this is what Marquardt has been encouraging. While the interests, beliefs, and principles held by historians – and even analysts or philosophers dealing with history – must not have the slightest of influence or interference in how events are explained or how they truly happened, historians should nonetheless avoid making people merely watch events parade by, for that would be nothing but wasting people's time, energy and mental acumen. Furthermore, if thinkers only present people with the events that have occurred, most people will assume that these events are what interpret all of the qualities, potentials, and faculties possessed by mankind. As a result, occurrences – which may even be tyrannical, wrong and oppressive – will be the basis on which people conclude "how human beings should be", "how the essence and nature of humanity is" and, as a consequence, "what human beings should do and how they should be"!

Fortunately, no conscious-minded, well-aware individual aiming to gain knowledge of what history presents us about mankind and human beings' potentials and capabilities will be satisfied with Ibn Khaldun's 6-volume work on history, *Kitāb al-Ibar wa-Diwan al-Mubtada wa-l-Khabar fi Tarikh al-Arab wa-l-Barbar wa-Man Asarahum min Dhawi ash-Shan al-Akbar* (*"Book of Lessons, Record of Beginnings and Events in the History of the Arabs and the Berbers and Their Powerful Contemporaries"*), which consists of almost 7000 pages; indeed, no one should deny the fact that the "hows" and "whys" regarding every event depicted in Ibn Khaldun's *Al-Muqaddimah* calls for research and further study. A significant part of *Al-Muqadimmah*, a book of Ibn Khaldun's which is over 580 pages in volume, has certainly been devoted to the narration of events. The rest of the book – perhaps no more than 200 pages – interpret and explain the almost 7000-page work described above. Now let us consider a researcher or a thinker busy studying a historical event in which human values and virtues contribute to the causes and the consequences of the event concerned. Let us assume that the thinker or researcher has gathered the highest amount of information possible regarding the event. Let us even assume that the thinker, an authority on the issue, has in fact witnessed every detail about the event with his own eyes, and no stone has been left unturned. Nonetheless, his work and all of the information and details included in it will merely be observations of physical effects of the event unless the thinker has enough passion and belief in supreme human values and virtues (provided, however, that he does not interpret and present them to his own advantage!). Thinkers and historians should not allow their work to be like that of sociologists who do nothing but see observable phenomena and gather statistical data which may have emerged as effects brought about by the social conditions, factors and relationships.

We must have in mind that not all of the selfish worshippers of worldly affairs or oppressors intoxicated with money or power who were involved – whether through their thoughts, their deeds, or their words – in the emergence of the Karbala event merely witnessed it happens without any awareness or information about the causes, circumstances or factors which brought about such a battle between good and evil; in fact, there were many people in Damascus and Kufa who were well aware of the important events that had occurred ever since the rise of Islam up to the Nainawa event, but – whether explicitly or implicitly, or maybe even through their silence – they neglected what Imam Hussain (PBUH) went through and actually allowed it to happen. The massive waves of shame, repentance, and the movements that arose in many parts of the Islamic communities of those days after the Imam was martyred, prove this. Therefore, historians researching the Karbala event cannot claim that the causes and incentives of this incident are unclear!

In any case, if an analytical study or interpretation of a major historical event is to be accurate and acceptable, it will not be enough to merely gain information and awareness about various aspects regarding the event. In fact, apart from being well-informed, a historian must make a distinction between good and evil; he should draw a line between justice and oppression and differentiate drowning in lusts and selfishness from piety and seeking divine moral ethics. In general, values and virtues need to be distinguished from anti-values and anti-merits. Conscious of the conflict between the issues mentioned above, historians should believe in goodness, justice, righteousness, piety and divine moral ethics. Otherwise, as we have already mentioned, their historical analyses and the accounts of history they provide will go no further beyond merely brushing the effects of events based on what has been seen or heard.

Part 4

The Third Introduction: Examples of Two Different Approaches Toward Historical Events

Let us now take the following examples, which include both kinds of approaches, into consideration.

1. When Mu'awiyah died, Walid ibn Utbah delivered the news to Imam Hussain (PBUH) and told the Imam that he was to pledge allegiance with Mu'awiyah's son, Yazid. While Walid had approached Imam Hussain (PBUH) gently and mildly in order to convince him about the allegiance, Marwan took a much more pharaoh-like, dictation-oriented stance and said, "It is my command that you must pledge allegiance with Yazid!" We must consider carefully who is giving such an order, and who the addressee is!

As Imam Hussain (PBUH) remarked:

> We belong to Allah, and we shall all return to Allah. It is time to bid Islam farewell and keep away from it [i.e., it is time to bid humanity farewell forever], for the Islamic population has been infected with a shepherd like Yazid.[14]

If one were, to sum up the order issued above by Marwan, a staunch Umayyad devotee, and the response by Imam Hussain (PBUH), considering his passion for Islam and its values and merits, merely based on the dialog between these two men, all one would conclude would be that Imam Hussain (PBUH) refused Marwan's offer, and was so astonished that he recited the verse of the Holy Quran regarding human beings' returning to Allah. Imam Hussain (PBUH) also commented on Yazid's absolute incapability for receiving his allegiance. The Quranic verse *"We belong to Allah, and we shall all return to Allah"* is normally quoted in cases of disaster or loss, and we are indeed facing a disaster here – a man like Yazid, totally ignorant of Islam and humanity, the man who wrote the following verses of poetry

> If only the great men of my tribe,
> who were killed in Badr,
> were here and could see how I took their revenge

---

[14] Shaikh Abbas Qumi (also known as Muhaddith Qumi), *Nafas ul-Mahmum.*

by killing the son of the Prophet of Islam and Ali... [15]

now plans to succeed the Holy Prophet and Imam Ali (Peace Be Upon Them) as the ruler of Islamic communities! The rise of Yazid, the son of Mu'awiyah, to power is equivalent to the demise of Islam. If an observer or a researcher studying the above statements has not understood what it means when the Holy Quran (The Family of Imran 3:19) states that *"The Religion before Allah is Islam [submission to His Will]"*, if one fails to comprehend the greatness of human beings trained and developed by Islam – such as Salman Farsi[16], Abu Dhar Al-Ghifari[17], Malik Ashtar[18], Ammar ibn Yasir[19], Uwais al-Qarani, Ibn al-Tayyihan[20], and Sa'id ibn Qais[21], each of whom are worth a whole evolutionary history, as well as thousands of other distinguished figures of sacrifice, mystical knowledge and great actions on the path of righteousness and justice – and if one fails to understand or accept the eternal logic of Islam when it comes to philosophy, worldview, various sciences, law, moral ethics, economy, politics, and culture from a general point of view, one will never be able to comprehend the fundamental damages caused by Yazid and the true meaning of depriving human beings of Islam.

2. A historian or an analyst of historical events may come across the statement *"If you have no faith in religion and you are not afraid of the afterworld either, [at least] you can live a free life in this world"*[22] in the context of the bloody tale of Hussain (PBUH) and understand to some extent what it means but the truth about it may be difficult to achieve. In order to comprehend the true meaning of the sentence, one must first realize the fact that the supreme goal of obeying religion and following the finest of human virtues is none other than making life and its values compatible to and dependent upon Allah. If some human beings degrade themselves from such a high level and thus deprive themselves of religion, they should at least

---

[15] Ibn al-Athir, *Al-Kamil fi Al-Tarikh ("The Complete History")*, Vol. 3. Also see Ibn al-Athir, *Usdul Ghabah Fi Marifat us-Sahabah*, Tabari's *Tarikh ("History")*, Vol.4, and at-Tirmidhi's *Sunan*, Vol. 13.

[16] Salman the Persian, also known as Salman al-Farsi, was a companion of the Holy Prophet (PBUH) and the first Persian who converted to Islam. [Translator]

[17] Abu Dhar Al-Ghifari was one of the early converts to Islam. [Translator]

[18] One of Imam Ali's most loyal companions. [Translator]

[19] Known for his dedication and devotion to the cause of Islam, Ammar ibn Yasir is regarded as one of the most loyal and most beloved companions of the Holy Prophet and Imam Ali. [Translator]

[20] Abu l-Haytham ibn al-Tayyihan was one of the Holy Prophet's and also Imam Ali's companions. He was a monotheist even before Islam. He was present at the wars of Badr, Uhud, and Khandaq. [Translator]

[21] Sa'id ibn Qais of Hamdan was a companion of Imam Ali and Imam Hassan ibn Ali. [Translator]

[22] Ibn Shu'ba Al-Harrani, *Tuhaf ul-Uqul ("The Masterpieces of the Mind")*

not forget about human honor and dignity and the importance of their following the principles of social life – most important of all, respect for human beings in times of peace. That is why the value of the statement above proves to be vague for those who are neglectful of the conscience of social life and its virtue.

3. Imam Hussain (PBUH), as historians all agree, addressed Yazid's corrupt men on the day of Ashura and said:

> *Beware that although that evil, adulterous man has put in the dilemma of whether to face the sword or being degraded and downtrodden, it is impossible for me to submit to the latter. Allah, His Messenger, faithful human beings and chaste souls will prevent us from succumbing to degradation and humiliation.*[23]

Imam Hussain (PBUH) has also said:

> *No! I swear to Allah that I shall never allow you to humiliate me, and I will never flee from jihad as slaves do [i.e., I will never admit that you are superior]. O servants of Allah! You may try to stone me, but I seek refuge from Allah, my Allah and yours, from the evils of any arrogant one who has no faith in Judgment Day.*[24]

The statements above make it possible for founders of true cultures and schools of thought to understand the supreme position and level human beings can achieve when it comes to honor, dignity and greatness. This is what mankind really means – a being who believes that a life of degradation, humiliation, and decadence is equal to death and is in fact quite distant from the dignity and honor Allah has blessed human beings with. Allah has not let man freely choose the quality of his life when it comes to dignity, honor, and values. In other words, no human being can claim, "I have total control and free will over my life. If I want to, I shall go on with my life, and if I wish to, I shall commit suicide and put an end to it!" The principle of life and continuing life with dignity and honor is Allah's decree; it is not a right that can be waived or transferred. This is the very point which has been neglected in the Universal Human Rights – the right to life, or in other words "the principle of life."

4. Indeed, any historian or writer may take into consideration and write an account of the story of Hur ibn Yazid Riahi's troops who were dispatched by Umar ibn Sa'd to capture Imam Hussain (PBUH) and take him to Kufa, but the most important human virtue underlying this story is easily neglected. Let us take a brief look at

---

[23] Shaikh Abbas Qumi (also known as Muhaddith Qumi), *Nafas ul-Mahmum*. Also see Ibn Abil-Hadid's *Sharh Nahjulbalaghah ("Commentary of the Nahjulbalaghah")*, Vol. 1.

[24] *Al-Alayli, Abdullah, Sumuw Al-Mu'nu Fi Sumuw Ath-That Aw Ashi'ah Min Hayat Al-Hussain ("The Loftiness of the Meaning in the Loftiness of the Essence, or Rays from the Life of Hussain")* and Shaikh Mufid, *Al-Irshad*, Vol. 2.

what happened:

> As Imam Hussain (PBUH) was passing by Sharaf on his way to
> Kufa, one of his men said, 'Allah-o Akbar!' 'Allah-o Akbar,' Imam
> Hussain (PBUH) repeated, 'but why did you say that?' 'I see palm
> trees ahead of us,' the man explained. 'There are no palm trees here,'
> the others said, 'all we see is horses and spears.' 'That is what I see as
> well,' Imam Hussain (PBUH) agreed.
>
> After some consultation, they headed toward Zi Khashab so as to
> avoid facing Hur's troops directly. Soon, the horses were in sight. We
> turned back, and when they saw us turn back, so did they. We got
> to Zi Khashab before they did. Imam Hussain (PBUH) told us to set
> up the tents. Hur's troops, about a thousand men, arrived; they were
> now facing Imam Hussain (PBUH) in that sweltering heat. Imam
> Hussain (PBUH) and his men had their turbans on and were armed
> with their swords. The Imam had his men provide Hurr's troops with
> as much water as they needed, and also splash water onto their horses
> to freshen them up. Imam Hussain's men filled bowls and basins
> with water, held them in front of each of the horses' mouths. Soon, all
> of the horses had drunk enough water.

Ali ibn Ta'an Muharibi has added:

> I was one of Hur's troops, and I was the last one to get there. When
> Imam Hussain (PBUH) saw that my horse and I were thirsty, he
> offered me the waterskin and said, "Tilt the tip of the waterskin,
> brother." I tried to drink some water, but the water would spill out
> of the waterskin. I didn't know what to do! Then Imam Hussain
> (PBUH), who had been watching, got up, came over to me and tilted
> the tip of the waterskin for me. Now I could drink water and give
> some to my horse as well."[25]

The value and significance of this great virtue are understandable only to
those who realize and believe in the right to human life and its dignity and
greatness beyond all friendships and animosities. Imam Hussain (PBUH)
must have known that these thousand troops would be tearing him apart
within a matter of days. Many thinkers and writers, from both the East and
the West, have written a great deal of material, expressed plentiful emotions
and produced evoking epics as an attempt to explore the fundamental roots
underlying the right to life, but none of them have had any success in solving
this divine secret, although they have presented useful material anyhow.
This great secret can be discovered only through an understanding of the
direct relation between life and Allah rather than superficial observations
and shallow knowledge accompanied by pre-fabricated principles instilled
in the mind!

---

[25] Shaikh Abbas Qumi (also known as Muhaddith Qumi), *Nafas ul-Mahmum*.

To further study this divine right as seen by Imam Hussain (PBUH), let us turn back to a few years prior to the bloody days of Nainawa, to the flames of war at Siffin, where the founders of Machiavellian[26] theories of that time had started a battle against Ali ibn Abi Talib (PBUH), Imam Hussain's father and a great pillar of truth and righteousness. During this war, history witnessed for the first time the divine right to life being observed and defended amazingly; as a result, a great philosophy was born – the philosophy of advocating and supporting life rather than worshipping it.

Now let us consider what happened during the battle. Mu'awiyah, the son of Abu Sufyan, had the Euphrates made unavailable to Imam Ali (PBUH) and his troops as an attempt to defeat tens of thousands of human beings by depriving them of water! He committed such a thoughtless act merely as an effort to fulfill his logic – "I want to dominate and be the boss, so I am the rightful, righteous one." Therefore, he set out to destroy tens of thousands of human beings' most deeply rooted right – their right to live – so as to enjoy his position of "I am the end, and others are the means" for a few more years and claim, "I can demand anything I want unconditionally" and "Whatever I want is righteous and appropriate!" Imam Ali's troops naturally found it hard to continue without any water, and thus they informed the Imam about the situation. Imam Ali (PBUH) ordered that the water of the Euphrates had to be available to all. His command was quickly obeyed, and the Muslims' problem about access to water – which had been brought about by a few so-called "Muslims" – was solved. Then, Imam Ali's troops decided to retaliate; they intended to ban Mu'awiyah's troops' access to the Euphrates to seek revenge for what they had done. Imam Ali (PBUH) – a man who had masterful knowledge of the "right to live", a man who lived by divine logic (that the aim of *jihad* is the betterment of humanity rather than the destruction of human beings) – however, did not allow his troops to cut off Mu'awiyah's men's access to water. He told his men:

> *Their right to live is not in our hands. Such a right has been created by Allah, and it is by Allah's will that the right to live meets its demise. Allow them to use the water.*

If a historian confines himself to merely collecting the physical effects of

---

[26] Niccolò di Bernardo dei Machiavelli (1469-1527), an Italian philosopher, stated that cunning, the voidance of dignity and dishonesty are the basic guidelines for life. He believed that a king is beyond any confinement or obligation commoners must observe. His theories can be summed up as: a) Seek benefit and advantage at all times. b) Respect no one but your own self. c) Do wrong, but pretend that you are doing good. d) Be greedy, and take as much as you can into your own possession. e) Be thrifty. f) Be savage and violent. g) Deceive others. i) Kill your enemies; even kill your friends. j) Use force when dealing with people. k) Put all of your efforts into battle. (See Thomas, Henry, & Thomas, Dana Lee, *Living Biographies of Great Philosophers*, and also Jafari, Muhammad Taqi, *A Translation and Interpretation of the Nahjulbalaghah*, Vol. 5.

the two events above (which the history of mankind has in its conscience regarding Imam Ali and Imam Hussain, two events that can contribute to human development) and not even provide a single word as an analysis or assessment of such events, he should ask himself and his conscience, "As a historian, how would you put these events together? It is like you are in a vast jungle, but all you have is a few leaves and a dry stick. You still happily think you have provided people with a history of mankind! How could a human being, with a sound mind and heart, gather all of these amazing, admirable or concerning events together and still neglect them!?"

Such historians should be aware that, by producing accounts of history in the manner mentioned above, they are in fact doing two things. First, they are drying out their hearts and brains quite neglectfully and hatefully in the face of the most effective acts of oppression and the most astounding cases of being oppressed. Secondly, they are also helping people get accustomed to being reckless, neglectful and ignorant regarding the hardships, tortures, and acts of tyranny afflicted upon the helpless and the oppressed!

Historians should fulfill the human mission they have undertaken and did mankind a service. By providing scientific conclusions based on the general consequences of historical events, they can fulfill their human duty – educating people values and anti-values in their individual or social lives.[27]

If the collection and the presentation of the history of mankind – with all of its ups and downs, the oppression and the downtrodden, the evolution and the falls of cultures and civilizations – are not used in order to develop man's current state and the future of mankind, all of the paper put into history books will be nothing but a waste; indeed, all of the energy, years of time and mental effort devoted to the production of these books will be a shame.

To complete this discussion, there is an important point that has to be made. Conscious-minded historians may encounter two kinds of values and anti-values when studying historical events.

The First Kind: The General Principles of Values and Anti-values

It is obvious that doing research upon and interpreting historical events of this kind will be by no means in conflict with the disposition and mindset of the historian, for, on one hand, realities and facts have been narrated in

---

[27] The greatest disadvantage, however, about putting events pertaining to human beings together has as seen by the humanities is that most physical behavioral effects emerging from human beings' actions are not confined to a single, specific reason; in fact, they may be brought about by several different causes. We read in accounts of history, for instance, that Iran and Greece have been at war on different occasions. These battles may have occurred due to economic reasons, vengeance, ideological conflicts, disputes regarding land, the arrogance of the rulers of the time, or greed for dominance. Nor which of the reasons mentioned above need to be taken into consideration in order to discover the truth about these wars?

detail, and on the other hand, interpreting and analyzing these facts based on general values and anti-values accepted by all human beings will prove to be a step forward when it comes to human development based on truths and observable facts. For example, when explaining the events about the emergence and rise of civilization, one would usually point out the reasons and circumstances behind it – a sound culture and economics, righteous judicial systems and effective education. If we claim that such accounts of history – i.e., accompanied by analyses and interpretations – is the greatest service one could provide man's "intelligible life" with, that would by no means prove to be an exaggeration. A study of the Holy Quran will show that the purpose of narrating all of the stories in this holy book is to educate mankind through presenting values and anti-values.

The Second Kind: Private Values and Anti-values regarding Specific Circumstances of Climate, Ethnicities, Cultures and Personal Events

Of course, there is no doubt that historians are under no obligation to express such values and anti-values; nonetheless, if they do so, there seem to be no factors preventing them from studying or interpreting them, either.

5.   Most of the existing accounts of the story of Imam Hussain's martyrdom have pointed out an amazing point. The more intense the conditions became as the day of Ashura drew closer to its critical hours, the more brilliantly Imam Hussain's face seemed to shine, and his spiritual flourish grew even stronger. Seeing the particular beauty expressed in his face, some of his closest companions remarked to one another:

Look at Hussain … he has absolutely no fear of death at all![28]

If one has undertaken the task of narrating and interpreting the history of mankind, when facing such inaccurate sources of history, should one not inform human beings that:

This is how immense the force of the human spirit is; even under the hardest of circumstances and the most horrific forms of suffering and torture, the human spirit can, aiming to excel in the competition for perfection, feel joy and flourish like the most triumphant one in the arena.

6.   Dear historians! If you write, or if you take into consideration books on the bloody tale of Imam Hussain (PBUH), you will come across an event that, despite seemingly insignificant, is in fact as immense as humanity itself. On Tasu'a night, Shimr bin Thiljawshan[29] – among the most wicked human beings ever – was dispatched by

---

[28] Shaikh Abbas Qumi (also known as Muhaddith Qumi), *Nafas ul-Mahmum.*

[29] Shimr bin Thiljawshan, a son of Thiljawshan, was from the tribe of Banu Kilab, one of Arabia's tribes. He is known as the man who killed Imam Hussain ibn Ali (PBUH) at the Battle of Karbala. [Translator]

Ubayd Allah ibn Ziyad[30], Yazid's staunch mercenary, to deliver a letter asking for When he shouted, quite near the tents, "Where are the children of our sister?" no one replied. Then Imam Hussain said, "You should answer [even though he is a wicked, evil man]." This response, as seen by human virtues, arises from the same divine source Imam Hussain's providing Hur and his troops – even their horses – with water does.

---

[30] Umayyad general and the governor for the Umayyad Caliphate in Kufa, Iraq, during the reign of Yazid I. [Translator]

Part 5

The Fourth Introduction: Unless Human Life Is Recognized Accurately and Its Supreme Goal Is Not Fully Explained, It Will, in Fact, Be the Lowliest and Most Degraded Phenomenon in All of Nature

If those in charge of a society do not take into serious consideration the issue of life and explaining and justifying it based on the supreme aim life has – in other words, if they leave people alone and let them merely understand and accept what their environment and incentives of selfishness and hedonism presents them with – how could such a life find an interpretation, a justification, or a principle preferable to death and oblivion?!

If only the majority of people would endeavor to defend spiritual values and "intelligible life" and bring about revolutions and changes with the same zeal and enthusiasm they go about, motivated and intrigued by political leaders, fulfilling their worldly needs and material desires. Then we would witness how elevated the greatness of human beings can truly become. It is this very historic wish that has led a great anthropologist to state:

> If only a small portion of the tears shed for people's hungry stomachs and unclothed bodies were shed for the souls and spirits longing for knowledge of human virtues and unclothed with garments of dignity and honor, there would remain neither a single hungry, bare spirit nor a hungry stomach or an unclothed body on earth.

A life without a criterion of righteousness or law, a life which regards no significance for what should be and what deserves to be, has thus been described by Allah in the Holy Quran:

> **They have hearts wherewith they understand not, eyes wherewith they see not, and ears wherewith they hear not. They are like cattle – nay, more misguided, for they are heedless [of warning].**[31]

Have you ever wondered how human beings – with all of their beauty, means for evolution and progress along the path of "intelligible life" – could degrade themselves even lower than animals?! It may not require a great deal of thought to understand that, because:

---

[31] The Heights (7:179)

1. Let us quote from Rumi:

    The fine questions which come to you from the supernatural
    should find their appropriate responses in the supernatural as well.[32]

By carefully considering the question, you will definitely find the answer.
You may ask, why are human beings equipped with all of their beauty and
all of the means, in order to achieve evolution and development along the
path of intelligible life? Why can they become even lower and more decadent
and degraded than animals?

The answer is quite clear: human beings, despite being endowed with
every means necessary for development and perfection, is prone to demise,
while animals do not even have access to such means.

2. The lowly state and ignorance of an animal, no matter how
    intense, will never be comparable to how ignorant or atrocious a
    wrongdoing, an oppressive human being may become.

All of the troubles and violations ever caused by animals on earth can
never be compared to the atrocity of a so-called "human being" like Genghis
Khan. When someone like Nero wishes that all people shared one single neck
so that he could behead all of them with one stroke of his sword, such an evil
intention expressed by an evil man like Nero could never be compared with
the violations or killings brought about by animals.

3. A snake has never been seen, heard, scientifically observed Abraham
    14:22ed or reported to have bitten a human being and then gone into
    its nest happily and rejoice with other snakes. No snake as ever said,
    whether in prose or poetry, to its prey, "Do you see how successfully
    I have defeated you?" Let us consider the following verse of poetry:

    Indeed, it was our man who, using his shiny, sharp-edged, Yemen-
    made sword,
    raised the head of your man on the day of battle!

4. Animals defend their food, habitat, and offspring to the extent that
    their survival necessitates; they may even kill to satisfy that need.
    Animals have never engaged in fights like mankind does – i.e.,
    based on baseless ideas or unfounded illusions. Indeed, as Rumi
    has put it:

    They make peace due to just an imagination, and then they start the
    war again.
    They cause disgrace owing to a mere hallucination.
    They act solely upon their imaginations and hallucinations. ...[33]

Unfortunately, hoarding items and commodities necessary for human
life, such as medicine, as an attempt to gain greater wealth and power, is

---

[32] Rumi's *Mathnawi*, Book 3.
[33] Rumi's *Mathnawi*, Book 1.

something seen only in human beings – who claim, quite brazenly, to be the most developed and complete living beings in the universe – rather than animals.

Now consider such a human-looking creature – which has been described by Allah as being even more decadent, lowly and degraded than animals – attempting to undertake, by means of the brutal force of his sword and along with a herd of his peers, the management of the Islamic society – a society in which the grounds and factors for the finest of human civilizations have been created by Muhammad (PBUH), the son of Abdullah, and presented the most civilized human beings possible – men like Salman Farsi, Abu Dhar Al-Giffari, Maytham al-Tammar[34], Malik Ashtar, Uwais Al-Qarni, Ammar ibn Yasir, Hujr ibn Adi[35], Amr ibn e Hamaq Al Khaza'i[36], great men who have been proved to have been the product of the logical and intellectual school of thought of Islam rather than their own personal characteristics – to the history of mankind.

How could Imam Hussain (PBUH) not have preferred to die with dignity and honor – which was, in fact, the flourish of his "reasonable life" – to continuing his life alongside those enemies of humanity? Indeed, had Imam Hussain (PBUH) decided to keep living a few more years in this world so as to be able to use earthly benefits and – due to his lack of disagreement with Yazid – enjoy the kindness of Yazid's flatterers most importantly of all, would he not have found himself ashamed in the presence of Allah?!

It is a pity how most people are not aware and conscious enough to understand the meaning of happiness and prosperity. With absolute simple-mindedness and complete ignorance of truths, they regard eating, drinking, sleeping, anger, lust, power and fame as being happiness and prosperity; thus, due to such a deviant image, they deprive themselves of true happiness. The divine logic Imam Hussain (PBUH) presented sees reaching the shores of life and entering the ocean of eternal life as opposed to living alongside tyrants and criminals; it is the former which can provide absolute happiness and prevent human beings from continuing to watch the stars, the sun, the moon and coexisting with human-looking anti-humans.

---

[34] Maytham ibn Yahya al-Tammar, more commonly known as Maytham al-Tammar, was an early Islamic scholar, a companion and disciple of Imam Ali (PBUH). [Translator]
[35] Hujr ibn Adi al-Kindi was a companion of the Holy Prophet Muhammad (PBUH). [Translator]
[36] A companion of the Holy Prophet (PBUH). [Translator]

Part 6

The Fifth Introduction: Human Life and Its Inherent Greatness and Dignity as Seen in Islamic Human Rights

a. Life is a blessing granted by Allah, and all human beings are guaranteed the right to life. All governments, all populations, and all individuals are obliged to support and safeguard the right to life against any violations or disturbances threatening natural life, such as diseases and natural disasters. No soul is to be separated from its body without the sufficient legal or religious causes to do so.

b. It is religiously prohibited to use any means, whether in general or in a specific way – to destroy or ruin the flow of human life.

c. Religion sees it mandatory to allow human life to go on as far as Allah allows it to, whether it be each individual's safeguarding one's life against harm from others or harm from oneself (e.g., suicide) or safeguarding others' lives.

d. Anyone who has been downtrodden or wrongfully harmed -- i.e., anyone whose life and dignity has been threatened due to natural factors or those in power – is required to rise up and make an attempt in order to eliminate the threat and safeguard his life and dignity in any legal way he is able to. On the other hand, anyone who does not fulfill this obligation has in fact assisted the oppressor in weakening him and threatening his life and dignity. As stated in the Holy Quran, when angels come across such people at the time of their deaths, they will be in a desolate, desperate, self-oppressed state:

> When angels take the souls of those who die in sin against their souls, they say, "In what [plight] were ye?" They reply, "Weak and oppressed were we in the earth." They say, "Was not the earth of Allah spacious enough for you to move yourselves away [from evil]?" Such men will find their abode in Hell; what an evil refuge![37]

---

[37] Women (4:97).

As we see in relevant parts of the Universal Declaration of Human Rights –
Articles 3 and 5, for instance – the necessity of human beings' safeguarding
their lives and also their right to drive away factors which may threaten or
weaken them have not received sufficient coverage.

Part 7

The Sixth Introduction: Islam Has Set Defending the Honor and Dignity of Life as One of Its Basic Principles, and Life Has Been the Purpose of the Amazing Event in Nainawa… But What Is Life?

A more general way to pose this question would be to ask, given the many battles and bloodsheds aiming to defend the dignity and honor of life the history of mankind has been riddled with, and the most important of which being the Karbala event: what is the nature and aim of life?

To discover the goal of life, we must first examine the nature of life and its immense qualities and specification to some extent.

The supreme aim of life is to be located within the attraction of divine perfection by means of conscious, free endeavors and efforts.

What do we mean by perfection? Perfection consists of the ability of a being to have the ultimate influence upon and be ultimately influenced by the universe, which is where Allah's wisdom and will are manifested.

Unfortunately, when clarifying the philosophy and purpose of life, the great nature and qualities of life are often neglected, and the issues pointed out to indicate that what they regard as life and pursue its knowledge and various aspects of its nature and features is, in fact, a vague issue including a number of phenomena, behaviors, and forces from birth to death!

Such a concept of life is obviously in contrast to the real nature, purpose, and qualities of which man tends to discover. Of course, in this introduction, we shall merely make a brief study of life and its purpose, for our aim is to prepare to evaluate the historic event in Nainawa.

The Nature of Life: Despite the fact that sciences and philosophies have not completely succeeded in discovering the nature of life, knowledge of the features of life has made a great contribution to man's progress in the two domains of "man as he is" and "man as he should be." We shall now provide instances of the features and qualities of life in order to further comprehend the immensity and the purpose of life:

1. There are many realities which may be employed in order to prove the greatness of life itself. We shall briefly point out just one thing. Gaining real knowledge of the essence of life requires seven million

questions posed by Oparin[38] in his work *Life, Its Nature, Origin, and Evolution* to be answered first.

As Oparin has stated:

> *It is only through such an evolutionary perception that we will be able to not only find out what goes on in the bodies of living things and why they occur in this way, but we will also manage to answer the seven million questions we encounter when attempting to discover what the true essence of life is.*[39]

Oparin states, however, in later parts of the book, that:

> *Unfortunately, our information is still too insufficient for us to be able to identify and define the path of this evolution systematically and take into consideration the qualitative changes and developments involved in the organized transfer of materials occurring in special phases of the evolution of the living world.*[40]

While studying Oparin's book, when I came across the former statement mentioned above, I noted, "If we also add the question why and how this evolution has started to the seven million questions mentioned here, that would make it seven million and one questions." Nonetheless, having read the latter statement of Oparin's mentioned above, I wondered why Oparin himself had not pondered the issue to a greater extent!

2. Man's mental endeavors and explorations and the creativity of the human mind has led to unimaginable scientific perfections and the emergence of thousands of fields of knowledge.

3. The emergence of the perfect virtues and aspects of superior worldviews and ideologies capable of directly proving that human life is dependent upon Allah; in fact, no worldview will be meaningful unless it provides a general remark on the universe, and no general remark will possible unless it has total knowledge and mastery over the universe and its principles and rules.

> *Our wisdom and reason will never be able to find dominance over the whole universe,*
> *for a reason is merely a part of the whole, and a part can never dominate the whole.*   (Naser Khusrow)

4. The human soul, endowed with unimaginable delicacy and tenderness, feels so powerful, resilient and resistant that it seems capable of withstanding the whole universe alone.

> *The "human self" can reach such a state of delicacy*

---

[38] Oparin, Alexander Ivanovich, Soviet biochemist noted for his theories on the origin of life. [Translator]

[39] Oparin, A.I., *Life, Its Nature, Origin and Evolution*.

[40] Ibid.

that it can even be influenced, for instance, saddened, by abstract beings (such as angels);
in other words, it cannot even bear the "self" of abstract angels.
Nonetheless, if love comes over a man, he can withstand the hustle and bustle of the universe.   (Hafiz)

We see, for example, Ali ibn Abi Talib (PBUH) – a man who, while highly sensitive about even pulling a piece of barley skin out of the mouth of an ant for fear of being oppressive, thus addresses the wrongdoers of his era:

> **I swear to Allah that I will feel no fear or horror even if I face all of them singlehanded, even if they fill the whole earth confronting me.**[41]

* * *

> **Even if you fill the land with your men in order to face me, I shall not escape; I will confront you.**

5. History has witnessed countless cases of amazing artistic genius in the form of various kinds of talents and potentials.
6. Cases of industrial genius, activities depicting extremely high precision and astounding examples of exquisitely fine work in various fields of technology which, having been achieved gradually along the path of the history of mankind, have not received as much recognition and appreciation as they deserve.
7. Various forms of reasonable, appropriate management of the plentiful existing civilizations and cultures, which depicts man's incredible capability to discover the fundamentals regarding humanity and the universe as well as man's ability to associate and match these basics with specific cases; all of these call for the finest of talents and the most supreme levels of genius.
8. High moral ethics, as well as elevated features in mystical and religious fields, have emerged in any society which has achieved human values to some extent throughout history. Although these great endeavors of the arena of "intelligible life" who competed against one another in good deeds and charitable efforts have taken up but a minor part of societies, they are nonetheless like the eyes, the brain or the heart of the body of mankind; they provide their communities with dignity and honor. They are the ones who can define the line between indulgence in natural animal life and "human intelligible life."

Since the immensity and the virtues mentioned here are emotional, those who achieve them cannot present their internal evolution and perfection to the people of their society in the form of physical effects. Therefore, ordinary people do not know that there are some amongst them who have succeeded,

---

[41] *Nahjulbalaghah,* Letter 66.

single-handedly, in activating the potential of making a great world within them. Indeed, evolutionary progress does not take place in physical aspects and is thus unobservable for the public. This is another kind of ascend.

> *If you become able to find yourself among those human beings who can ascend mystically,*
> *you will easily be capable of definitely eliminating yourself [i.e., abstracting yourself] from natural interests thus, finding feathers to rise toward the highest of worlds.*[42]

(Rumi is not implying moving on the earth or traveling to the moon; he is referring to evolution from the lowly state of animals up to the highest levels of humanity – which he here resembles the transformation of sugar cane into sugar.)

> *The lips of a true mystic are sealed [i.e., he has taken a vow of silence], even though he has a myriad of hidden secrets inside him.*
> *A mystic's lips are silent, but his heart is filled with calls from the supernatural.*
> *Mystics who have taken a sip from the divine cup of secrets get to know some of those secrets, but they do not reveal anything to others, for if anyone learns such secrets, their lips will be sealed with silence as well.*
> *[In other words, one who achieves divine secrets is not allowed to share such secrets with others.]*[43]

Such virtues and spiritual values emerge when those who have achieved them come across events which reveal their inner virtues and characteristics.

Most often, great faculties and virtues of the human spirit do not emerge during a human being's life – unless events occur in the society and make great human beings feel the obligation to determine their stance from a certain aspect or aspects. In such cases, man's great values and virtues may emerge socially. Let us consider Abu Dhar al-Ghifari, for instance. Before economic and cultural disorders had arisen in Islamic societies, he was a pious man of faith – perhaps known to the public as a good, average Muslim. That is, of course, before lawfulness and orderliness – which has been described in the Quran as following the verse *"Verily the most honored of you in the sight of Allah is [he who is] the most righteous of you"*[44] – was blurred by racist tendencies, lust for power and selfishness (which was one of the factors leading to the occurrence of the Karbala event). It was at that point when Abu Dhar began experiencing a storm inside him, an outpour which to some extent introduced him to the people of his society. Before that, people knew nothing about how Abu Dhar felt inside about human lives and the value of the work done by people. This great man's life was, however, coming to an end

---

[42] Rumi's *Mathnawi*, Book 4.

[43] Ibid, Book 5.

[44] The Apartments (49:13).

in that desert of Al-Rabadha – where he had been exiled to. All of a sudden, the grave anxiety his dear wife was experiencing brought his attention back to this world. He asked his passionate, sympathetic companion in this world what was worrying her. "Now that you are soaring up toward eternity," his wife replied, "what will become of me, all alone in this appalling abyss?"

"Look at that road over there," Abu Dhar replied. "That black spot is a group of travelers on their way to Madina. When I have died, go to the side of the road and tell them a man, a Muslim, a companion of the Holy Prophet (PBUH) has died here. They will come and bury me after going through the rituals required. They will also take you to Madina, back to your family."

At that moment, the ocean of human virtues inside Abu Dhar produced another powerful wave, and he displayed another act which showed how important human life is. "My dear wife," he said, moments before his death, "when they come to my dead body and are going to fulfill their religious-human obligations, and prepare me for my move toward eternity, tell them that Abu Dhar insisted that they slaughter and eat that sheep, the only thing I have in my possession now, and then begin washing my body and burying me. They should not do anything for me without being rewarded for it."

Indeed, it was this very knowledge of the value of human life, emerging from the Quranic verse:

> *Give just measure and weight, nor withhold from the people the things that are their due.*[45]

Which found its way into Abu Dhar's perfection-seeking spirit, and also busied the minds of great men like Ibn Khaldun and David Ricardo during later periods of history. If only there were another man like Abu Dhar who would present mankind with the true meaning of work. Oh, Allah! How did these achievers of perfection see life and the aim of life that made them able to soar up so much? How could such people prefer to live alone in the desert in Al-Rabadha rather than socialize with people who had lost their own souls? As Rumi has written, in order to understand the truth about life and the aim of life:

> *O, Lord! The events occurring in this world are dark and distressing; bestow upon us insight sharp enough for us to avoid the traps of this world.*
> *O, Lord! Make us capable of distinguishing the dust covering the realities from the realities themselves;*
> *Grant us the insight that can save us from such a perilous darkness [i.e., the dark surrounding the truth about life].*[46]

Divine mentors have advised that in order to achieve internal enhancement of character (the most important elements of which fall out of man's free

---

[45] The Heights (7:85), Hud (11:85), and The Poets (26:183).
[46] Rumi's *Mathnawi*, Book 6.

will), besides the natural endeavors man needs to take into consideration, he also has to take into account supernatural elements if he is to discover the best path of life possible in the natural world. Man must know that Allah can help him adjust the involuntary elements of his "self" both directly and indirectly so that he can identify any traps along his path. In other words, traps will look tiny and meager, the darkness will be passable thanks to the light within man, and the whirlpools which suddenly arise in life will show their true face and man will thus be able to take a different path to avoid them. Even if a man fails to see the whirlpool in advance, and is thus unable to change his path and avoid it, man will joyfully face the whirlpool. To be able to achieve insight, man needs to have in mind that despite all of the powers he has, he nonetheless lies in the field of the dominance of a divine being; he is, in fact, a mere part of the whole calculated plan of the universe.

Let us avoid all jargons invented by various isms and schools of thought whose founders and speakers have no inkling about what *"We have honored the sons of Adam"*[47] means; instead, we should follow Imam Hussain (PBUH) and his eternal logic – *"Indeed, we are far from any abjection or ignominy"* – in order to purify and refine mankind from all of the evils of abasement. Unless we abide by the principle depicted in the Quranic verse mentioned above (*"We have honored the sons of Adam"*), the heavy burden of abjection will leave us no chance for an intelligible life. If one human being dies, we merely feel sad; if millions of human beings die in the arena of the fight for survival, we will just fill pages with statistics. Now we shall continue with our discussion on life and understand its greatness:

9.   To illustrate how great the flourish of life is, it would suffice to mention the astounding acts of sacrifice aiming to defend human souls and spirits as well as human values such as dignity, honor, and intelligible freedom.

10. The intuitive reception of amazing truths about beauty and greatness in the human soul has become the main axis for religious pioneer culture and civilized peoples in the world.

Have you ever pondered the fact that a book of poetry has pointed out, on 6300 occasions, details about the nature of life, its characteristics and its values in the finest form possible?[48]

Moreover, as Attar has written:

> *In this vast universe, no sound, no movement, even no stationary object, is purposeless.*
> *Any particle or galaxy you look at, whether the tiniest living thing or man, the most perfect of them all,*
> *is busy in this magnificent universe,*
> *even though none is aware of the state others are in,*

---

[47] The Holy Quran, The Night Journey (17:70)
[48] Rumi's *Divan-e Shams*.

they even know nothing about their own state.[49]

*   *   *

What a bride exists in the soul,
the picture of whose face has decorated The Universe
like brides' tender, delicate hands![50]

When Rumi states that:

The direction the soul should take is hidden,
and that is why each human being heads toward a different direction.[51]

He is, in fact, attempting to help us understand the Quranic verse **"Whithersoever ye turn, there is the presence of Allah."**[52] Thus, people are quite varied when it comes to internal activities such as imaginations, associations, decisions, thoughts, etc. regarding the origins of creation. In other words, although we are unable to achieve complete scientific or sensory discovery of the roots of the fundamental activities and mental endeavors of human beings, it seems that all of these internal differences cannot all be attributed to differences in external factors and motives. If all human beings had equal contact with these factors and motives, there would be no differences among human beings' imaginations, associations, thoughts, self-awarenesses, wills, decisions, etc.

We should also have in mind that endeavoring to understand the aim of life through science and philosophy, although advantageous, will have us dealing only with limited concepts and propositions – most of which are based on effects rather than causes.

Therefore, we should find a way to make use of the eighth (the moral, religious, mystical and ethical virtues achieved by endeavours of the path of intelligible life) and ninth (the amazing, selfless acts of sacrifice made in order to defend human lives, mankind and the values of humanity) items discussed above in order to gain knowledge of life, its greatness and its supreme goal, for they are – and only they are – the ones which show us how the physical phenomena of life can be surpassed on to achieve true life.

Allah knows that a mystical pilgrim needs love and passion in order
to achieve his goal;
reason and ration are of no help on this path.[53]

---

[49] Farididdin Attar Neishabouri, *Mantiq it-Tair*.

[50] Rumi's *Divan-e Shams*.

[51] Rumi's *Mathnawi*, Book 5.

[52] The Cow (2:115).

[53] Rumi's *Mathnawi*, Book 1.

Part 8

The Seventh Introduction: A Discussion on the Five Principles of Power, Good and Evil

One of the most important lessons mankind can learn from the constructive movement of Imam Hussain (PBUH) regards the definition and true interpretation of power – unfortunately, pioneers and those in charge of the cultural, political, moral and religious management of societies have not provided people with enough education on this issue. Had human societies really been supplied with training on what power really means, original cultures and political principles which educated people on "intelligible life" would not have lost their core and their true meaning to the Machiavellians of their eras; not would make religious truths and moral ethics – which are in charge of human evolution and development – have become so inefficient. This [so-called] calamity is not so hidden that detailed explanations and extensive reasoning will be required to prove it. Therefore, we shall now present and discuss five important principles regarding power, righteousness, and evil.

Principle 1: Power, in Any Form, Is the Driving Force of All Changes

In any form it may be, power is what brings about changes and movements, thus causing the emergence and survival of the realities of the universe. In such a sense, power is regarded as one of the most original and most significant factors in creation, for it makes things come into being and prevail. Therefore, power is a truth which has innate value.

Principle 2: In One Sense, Power is an Unconscious Truth

When in the hands of a human being, power is activated at the will of the human being; thus, power will not only have any free will of its own, but it will also be unaware of its fate as well. We shall provide further explanation on this issue below.

The unawareness of power in what it does is quite obvious in the realm of observable, physical realities, such as the various kinds of power in nature and also the different forms of energy which can be regarded, from one point of view, as examples of forces. The forces and energies existing and active in nature, whether causing construction or destruction, do not do what they do knowingly; they have no previous strategies, free will or self-consciousness. The unawareness and lack of free will of power when it comes to various fields of science and activities carried out by man, however, lies in its dependence upon the management of the human being using it. Thus, now the value of power depends on what the holder of the power is aiming it at.

Principle 3: Power Is Essentially a Manifestation of Righteousness and Good

Given the two principles above, those who constantly regard power as conflicting with righteousness – and always ask, "Is power the triumphant one or righteousness?" – In fact, understand neither of power nor righteousness. As we have pointed out, power is a significant appearance of righteousness, and it is mankind who can use it in the most constructive ways or to serve the most destructive purposes. Thus, power will never become the enemy of righteousness.

Power, being an example of truth, cannot turn against righteousness; likewise, evil will never be a match for righteousness, either. For instance, let us suppose that all of the evil powers and evil forces in the world come together and claim that, "Thinking is bad! There is no need to pay employees with wages! Ignorant, stupid people can manage a society! The light and the dark are the same! There is no difference between knowledge and ignorance!" Can all of the evil powers and evil-doers in the world change the truth about these things? That is impossible.

Principle 4: It is the Advocates of Right and the Advocates of Wrong Who Place Themselves in Conflict with One Another, Not Power, Righteousness and Evil Per Se

It is a fact that – throughout history – the lustful greedy and the selfish have enjoyed a group of supporters who believe that the only important things are their own lusts, desires and selfish interests. On the other hand, there are other human beings who – due to their conscious character, elevated morals and knowledge – advocate the truth and righteousness, no matter how hard or painful it may be, when it comes to answering the six main questions: Who am I? Where have I come from? Why am I here? Where am I now? Who am I with? Where do I go from here?

The two groups mentioned above (i.e., those who support righteousness and those who advocate evil) have been in constant battle and conflict, whether in private or in public, throughout history and in all societies. Whichever side that achieves natural power defeats the other. In other words, the two groups confronting and killing one another are in fact two groups of human beings; one group supports good and righteousness and the other group advocates evil. Righteousness, evil and power do not directly engage in battle themselves. If the supporters of evil lose, evil might emerge once again (even though it has not succeeded), and if the supporters of good and righteousness fail, it will be a superficial defeat, for righteousness and good lies superior to and beyond such confrontations. Therefore, even if the greatest martyr of all humanity – Imam Ali or Imam Hussain, for instance

– set foot on the battlefield, were defeated and martyred a thousand times, they would never be defeated, for their ideal is righteousness. Such men are triumphant forever because righteousness is victorious for good. Let us consider some of the words of Imam Hussain (PBUH), this great martyr of the path of righteousness:

> *In the Name of Allah, the Compassionate, the Merciful.*
> *This is a letter from Hussain, the son of Ali, to Muhammad, the son of Ali, and other offspring of Hashim. Whoever joins me will be a martyr, and whoever defies me will not achieve triumph.*[54]

Likewise, those who kill such martyrs will never achieve victory, either. As Al-Uzri[55] has written:

> *"Swords may have mutilated the martyrs of the bloody plain of Nainawa,*
> *but their spiritual greatness and their virtues remained intact…"*

We can conclude that there is no innate direct conflict or man-to-man battle between righteousness, evil and power essentially.

Principle 5: The Power to Harness and Control One's Internal Desires and Whims Is the Greatest and the Most Valuable Power of All

Let us indicate the significance of this issue in one sentence and sincerely devote our attention to understanding it. Then, we can set about realizing the relevant pains and cures in our social lives. Du Pasquier has said:

> *Since mankind was unable to regard justice as power and see the just as powerful, power is seen as justice, and the powerful are considered to be just.*[56]

To such a meaningful sentence, which arises out of its speaker's awareness of a pitiful phenomenon, we must add that there is another incapability which is even more unpleasant and more distressing than that depicted in the statement above – man still has no tendency to admit to this incapability so that he may take measures to resolve it! The above statement may be quite appealing, but its content can also be rephrased as human beings have submitted themselves to power rather than justice.

This truth, which has emerged from psychological observations and experiences past and present, calls for more serious attention: if a human being incapable of controlling his own ego encounters something and finds passionate interest in it, the object may not only possess that human being

---

[54] Muhammad ibn Qawlawayh, *Kamil Al Ziyyarat.*

[55] Abd al-Hussayn Al-Uzri (1880-1954) was an Iraqi poet. [Translator]

[56] Du Pasquier, Claude (1937): *Introduction À la Théorie Génàrale Et la Philosophie du Droit*, Paris. Some quotations from the Holy Prophet and his progeny have also included the same concepts of this sentence, albeit in varied forms.

but also take charge of his being and his goals. As Rumi has written:

> *The body parts we human beings are made of consist of nothing but*
> *bones and natural flesh;*
> *what accounts for the humanity in man, however, is thought.*
> *Take thought away from mankind and there will be merely physique.*
> *Think about flowers, and inside you will be like a garden of flowers*
> *in bloom.*
> *If you think of thorns, however, you will be like wood only useful for*
> *burning for heat.*[57]

Furthermore, as depicted in the following verses by Mulla Muhsen Feyz Kashani:

> *If a man continually ponders the whole within his own self and take*
> *this endeavor seriously,*
> *divine light will begin to shine on him.*

When a man is intensely affected by something, the mental aspect of the subject overwhelms the depths of the elementary levels of man and then proceeds like an active spiritual element, leading to actions and activities similar to the element itself. Some scholars even believe that the intensity of the influence an issue on the "human self" causes the "self" to feel a sort of unity between itself and the issue.

Thus, the humanity of human beings lies not in physical components or ornaments making the physique beautiful but in man's mental and spiritual state. Without thought and intellect, there will be no criterion left for humanity. It is thought and intellect which makes man different from other beings and opens the infinite path of perfection before him. In other words, to evaluate and assess human beings, it is only thought and ways of thinking which need to be taken into consideration.

The feeling of being identical to something that we have a passion for originates from human beings' attraction toward their beloved; the deeper that attraction is, the more intense the imagination or perception of being the same as the beloved will be. When encountering power, if human beings had not gotten carried away and become helpless, if they had controlled their egos and took charge of their actions reasonably, the course of history would have proven to be the true evolution of human beings rather than the natural progress of history which, unfortunately – thanks to the emergence of highly appealing and very useful technologies – has also taken a fake concept of civilization as well![58]

Now we can see, to a considerable extent, why it is extremely destructive to lose oneself regarding power and become intoxicated with it, for a conscious truth – the human character and personality – must not become

---

[57] Rumi's *Mathnawi*, Book 2.
[58] Jafari, Muhammad Taqi, *A Translation and Interpretation of the Nahjulbalaghah*, Vol. 5.

totally captivated by an unconscious, flowing truth for actions – natural power. Power is in constant transformation and flows for activity and action, particularly if it falls into the hands of those who have lost themselves to power in order to gain it. Even the painful cries of those begging for help, even the mere weakness of the meek, is tempting to them. Therefore, the more intensely those in possession of power submit themselves to it, the greater the destructive of power will be. Let us consider the crimes Yazid committed: the massacre he had Muslim bin Aqaba make in Madina, his insults to the sacred House of Allah in Macca, his having the Kaba hit by catapults and burned down[59], and his recitation of poetry by Ibn Al-Zabi'ra when Imam Hussain's head was brought to him:

> If only the great men of my tribe, who were killed in Badr,
> we're here today to see how fatal my blow has been!
> If they could see this scene, they would be delighted and excited.
> 'Well done, Yazid!' they would tell me.
> We killed the most prominent of them; now we are even
> when compared to the event in Badr.
> Hashim's clan played with the kingdom and power;
> Allah has had no hand in this, and there has been no revelation,
> either.
> I cannot be considered as a member of the Khindif clan
> unless I seek vengeance for what Ahmad's offspring have done.

Another example to consider is the pledge he had the residents of Madina make to be his slaves.[60] Is all of this wickedness, blasphemy, and tyranny not enough to prove the evil in being possessed by and submitting oneself to power?!

---

[59] Razi Qazvini, Abdul Jalil, *Kitab al-Naqz ("The Book of Refutation")*.

[60] For further reading on these wicked acts, see Al-Masudi's *Muruj-ul Thahab ("Meadows of Gold")*, Vol. 3; Al-Suyuti's *Tarikh ulKhulafa ("The History of the Caliphs")*; Ibn Qutaybah al-Dinawari's *al-Imama wal-Siyasa*, Vol. 1; Dinawari's *Al-Akhbar al-Tiwal ("General History")*; Al-Dinvari's *Al-Akhbar* Yaqubi's *Tarikh* Yaqubi, Vol. 2; Al-Halabi's *Al-Sirat ul-Halabiyyah*, Vol. 1; Al-Tabari's *Tarikh Al-Tabari*, Vol. 4; Al-Jawzi's *Tathkiral Khwas*; Ibn al-Athir's *Al-Kamil fi al-Tarikh*, Vol. 3; Ibn Abi l-Hadid's *Sharh Nahjulbalaghah ("Commentary of Nahjulbalaghah")*, Vol. 3.

Part 9

The Eighth Introduction: The Two Basic Pillars of Characters Who Build the Pioneer Culture of Humanity – Both of Which Imam Hussain (PBUH) Had in Their Highest Form

The First Pillar: Hereditary Factors

The Second Pillar: Developmental and Environmental Factors

If a character capable of building the pioneer culture of mankind is to be generated and activate, two basic factors are required. It is agreed on by scholars of the humanities that – as a principle, or a law of the formation and organization of the character – the elements of each human being's character take shape early in life; fixed elements and principles are acquired and formed inside human beings by means of exposure and contact with both external and internal realms, and as human beings go through the ups and downs of the path of life, the elements of their characters are activated and managed. Due to his greatness and original nature, Imam Hussain (PBUH) had perceived his fixed elements and principles from both internal and external realms.[61]

   a.   Internal Realms: When it comes to chastity and purity, Imam Hussain's parents and grandparents were incredible sources to inherit from. As we read in the seventh prayer for a pilgrimage to Imam Hussain's shrine:

> O, Master! O Aba Abdillah! I give witness that you were pure and chaste from the very beginning of your conception, and you were conceived by pure parents. Ignorance and decadence were unable to contaminate or deceive you.[62]

Thus, it can be stated that Imam Hussain's progress was, in fact, the domain of the same divine, brilliant flow toward eternity which he had gone through before entering natural formation. This has been depicted in the following verses of poetry:

> The spirit and soul within man brought me to you [Allah];
> I have gone through long and different paths in order to reach you.
> (Nayyer Tabrizi)

*   *   *

> The supreme goal human beings are heading for,
> from the time, they are non-existent and through all the stages of

---

[61] A question may arise here, and it must not be left unanswered. If a character sets foot onto this world innately free of the possibility of being contaminated by animal evils and wickedness, why will it need education and development now that it has entered the universe with a matured, developed personality already? We can respond by saying that purity, divine enlightenment and chastity involves seeds being planted inside such characters; later on, Allah-sent leaders, common sense and pure conscience helps these seeds grow and flourish. Such characters are not born with activated, developed virtues. The following statements of Imam Ali's (quoted from Sermon 192 of *Nahjulbalaghah*) provide clear proof for this: "You know how intimate I was with the Holy Prophet (PBUH). When I was a child, he would seat me on his lap and keep me close to his chest. At night, he would allow me to lie beside him. The fragrance of his blessed body would caress my nose. Sometimes he would bless something with his mouth and then give it to me to eat. He never heard me tell a lie or do anything wrong. Ever since he was weaned, Allah had the greatest of His angels guide the Holy Prophet along the path of the finest virtues and moral ethics in the world. I did whatever he did, like a baby camel following its mother. Every day, he would present me with a new aspect of morals and ethics, and then he would tell me to observe it and follow it …"

The statements above vividly indicate the effect of education and development in the activation of the innate virtues Imam Ali and the Holy Prophet had been endowed with.

[62] Safwan Jammal, *Misbah*, quoted by Muhaddith Qumi.

existence,
is nothing but passion for achieving the final place of love…
(Hafiz)

b. External Realms, regarding the family and environment Imam Hussain (PBUH), was born and raised in – a clan managed by the Holy Prophet (PBUH) with the assistance of Imam Ali (PBUH), as well as Fatima Zahra (PBUH) as his mother and Imam Hassan Mujtaba (PBUH) as his brother. At that time, the pioneer culture of Islam and its newly established civilization had set "objective, intelligible life" as its main axis. During the period of his life in which the human character is formed, Imam Hussain (PBUH) lived with the greatest examples of justice, human virtues and the finest of moral principles provided for him by the Holy Prophet, Imam Ali and his mother Fatima (Peace Be Upon Them). Therefore, he had such great passion and faith in justice and elevated virtues that doubt or ignorance toward them would be like being ignorant toward the supreme aim of life itself. From the four great human beings he had grown up with and been brought up by, he had learned that life is equal to death without its supreme goal, and from another point of view, an honorable, dignified death cannot only be superior to an aimless life but can also save conscious, virtuous human beings from a decadent, baseless effort known as life! This is not an unfounded, crude feeling. The significance of education and development in the greatness of righteousness, the need to make life righteous, the wickedness of evil and the importance of avoiding it can be quite clearly seen in Imam Hussain's goals, deeds, and words. Let us take an example into careful consideration:

> *Do you not see that righteousness is downtrodden and evil is not avoided?*
> *It is at such times when faithful people, although acting rightfully and doing good, wish to meet their makers.*
> *In such circumstances, I regard death as emancipation, whereas living alongside wrongdoers is nothing but depressing, painful boredom."*[63]

Indeed, when righteousness and good have been eliminated from people's lives, and evil is not avoided, what is left of life and what life truly means?

The need to accept such a belief and act absolutely righteously is the very logic presented by the Quran, which Imam Hussain (PBUH) not only completely knew, but also witnessed in all of the words, deeds, and goals of the great human beings he was brought up by. Thus, through the greatest

---

[63] Al-Sayyid Mustapha Al Ul-I'timad, *Lum'at min Balaghat al-Hussain: Khulub, Rasa'il, Mawa'iz*, Karbala, A'la Publications. Also see Shabrawi's *Al-Ittihaf*, Abu Na'im's *Hilyat ul-Owlia*, Vol. 2, and Farhad Mirza's *Qamqam*.

of efforts, he succeeded in activating his innate, brilliant nature and essence and nature.

To sum up, it can be stated that early into his blessed life, living alongside true sources of Islam, Imam Hussain lived a life of consciousness and awareness, and through his sharp perception and sound sense, he had realized what a life-saving blessing his grandfather Muhammad ibn Abdullah had brought for mankind. When the Holy Prophet (PBUH) was receiving revelations from Allah – indeed the closest form of contact possible between Allah and a servant of His – Imam Hussain (PBUH) would watch the divine, brilliant face of his grandfather and stock away within himself the most stable requirements for an objective, intelligible life.

Imam Hussain (PBUH): Established and Accepted by the Whole Islamic Community as the Greatest Character of His Time

For further reading about the immense character of Imam Hussain (PBUH) as depicted in acclaimed Islamic sources, readers are encouraged to refer to *Rays of the Greatness of Hussain (PBUH)* by the respectable scholar Lutfullah Safi. I believe this book is one of the most comprehensive works of research on how great Imam Hussain's character was.

We shall now take a look at the confessions made by figures who not only did not belong to the school of thought of Imam Ali but they, in fact, opposed it to some extent.

There is plentiful historical evidence that Imam Hussain (PBUH) was the most popular man of his era. Obviously, a part of people's affection for him lay in his being the Holy Prophet's grandson and Imam Ali's son. On the other hand, it was also due to the perfected virtues accumulated in his character; some of these virtues showed themselves in the incredible way he managed the Karbala event. Let us now go through some of these historical pieces of evidence:

1. When Walid bin Utbah invited Imam Hussain (PBUH) so that Walid could give him the news of Mu'awiyah's death and get him to make a pledge of allegiance to Yazid:

    > Imam Hussain said, 'I do not suppose you will be satisfied if I make a pledge of allegiance with Yazid in secret. You want it to be done publicly, for all to know about it.'
    > 'Yes, that is so,' Walid replied.
    > 'Then when morning comes,' Imam Hussain said, 'you will find out what my opinion is.'
    > Walid answered, 'Then go back, in the name of Allah, and come back to us along with the people.'
    > 'I swear to Allah,' Marwan told Walid, 'If you let Hussain leave now without having him make that pledge of allegiance, you will never be able to get him to do it, not without a great many people getting killed. Do not allow him to leave before you have him make his pledge

of allegiance to Yazid. If he does not, behead him.'

Hearing this, Imam Hussain rose and said to Marwan, 'O, son of the woman with blue eyes! Are you going to kill me? Or is he going to do it? You lied, so you have sinned.' Then Imam Hussain left for his home along with his relatives and his friends.

'You didn't take my advice,' Marwan told Walid. 'I swear to Allah, with that character he has, he will never give in to you.'

'You are leading me toward an event that will destroy my faith and religion,' Walid replied. 'I swear to Allah that I would not accept the whole world to be mine if it were at the expense of killing Hussain. Why should I kill Hussain just because he won't pledge allegiance? I swear to Allah, I know that whoever is judged based on Hussain's blood on Judgment Day will have barely any deeds worthy of assessment when facing Allah.'[64]

2. Mu'awiyah had given Yazid advice about the men Mu'awiyah feared might attempt to take charge after his death. Regarding Imam Hussain, Mu'awiyah had said:

   Hussain, however, is a man of a powerful, exciting spirit. The people of Iraq will not leave him, so you will not face him alone. If you overcome him, leave him alone, for he is a relative of ours, and he is also closely related to and was quite close to Muhammad.

3. As Abbas al-Aqqad[65] has written:

   Hussain lived for 57 years. He had enemies who would go out of their way to lie to get an advantage over him, but they could never find fault in Hussain. They never succeeded in denying Hussain's great virtues. Even when Mu'awiyah received Hussain's condemning letter and those close to Mu'awiyah insisted that he should write back and threaten Hussain. Mu'awiyah said, 'When it came to Ali, maybe I had something to use to make false accusations and raise suspicions about him, but I have nothing to accuse Hussain of to do that.[66]

The deceiving Mu'awiyah is implying the lies he spread about how Uthman got killed – a conspiracy Mu'awiyah was involved in himself whereas Imam Ali (PBUH) had nothing to do with it.

4. Kharazmi[67] has also written in his book *Maqtal al-Hussain*:

   When Walid bin Utbah heard that Imam Hussain (PBUH) had left

---

[64] Muhaddith Qumi, *Nafas ul-Mahmum*.

[65] Abbas Mahmoud al-Aqqad (1889-1964), Egyptian journalist, poet and literary critic, and member of the Academy of the Arabic Language in Cairo. [Translator]

[66] Al-Aqqad, Abbas Mahmoud (1963): *Al-Hussain: Abu al-Shuhada ("Hussain: The Father of Martyrs")*.

[67] Al-Muwaffaq ibn Ahmad ibn Muhammad al-Makki al-Khawarizmi (d.568 AH).

for Iraq, he wrote Ubayd Allah bin Ziyad a letter. 'Hussain, the son of Ali, has set out for Iraq,' he wrote. 'He is the son of Fatima, the Prophet's daughter. O son of Ziyad! Avoid hurting him, for that would lead to consequences in this world which no one could ever prevent and no one would ever be able to forget.

5. When Hamzah bin Mughirah bin Shu'bah learned that his uncle Umar ibn Sa'ad had decided to fight Imam Hussain (PBUH), Hamzah thus warned his uncle:

    I seek refuge with Allah, for you have decided to battle Hussain, thus opposing Allah and putting away all compassion and mercy. I swear to Allah that losing everything there is to own in the whole world, all the property and power there is, would be better than facing Allah with Hussain's blood on your hands.[68]

6. Following the Karbala event, those who had killed Imam Hussain were hated, damned and condemned by people in all communities.
7. Abdullah al-Alayli has thus described Imam Hussain:[69]

    Hussain was popular among all people; he enjoyed a special standing among all different groups and classes of people. He had such charisma that everyone believed that he was sacred. The public saw him as higher than ordinary people.

8. One day, Abdullah bin Umar[70] was sitting in the shade of the Kaaba when he saw Hussain (PBUH). "This man," he said, "is the most popular man both on the earth and also in the heavens."[71]
9. To refute Abu Bakr ibn al-Arabi Al-Maliki[72] -- who had claimed that "Hussain was killed due to his own grandfather's canonical and religious law" – Abdul Rahman Ibn Khaldun has written:[73]

    The judge, Abu Bakr ibn al-Arabi was wrong about what he said regarding Hussain. This mistake was because the judge did not

---

[68] Al-Tabari, Muhammad ibn Jarir, *Tarikh al-Rusul wa al-Muluk ("History of the Prophets and Kings")*, often referred to as *Tarikh Al-Tabari*, Vol. 4. Also see Ibn Al-Athir's *Al-Kamil fi al-Tarikh ("The Complete History")*, Vol. 3.

[69] Abdullah al-Alayli's Sumuw Al-Ma'na Fi Sumuw Ath-That Aw Ashi'ah Min Hayat Al-Hussain ("The Loftiness of the Meaning in the Loftiness of the Essence, or Rays from the Life of Al-Hussain").

[70] Abdullah ibn Umar (614-693) was the son of the second Caliph Umar. [Translator]

[71] Ibn Hajar al-Asqalani, *al-Isaba fi tamyiz al-Sahaba*, Vol. 1.

[72] A jurisprudential scholar of the "Dhahirin" (a school of jurisprudence who merely took superficial content into consideration) and a man of many works and accomplished, he is not to be mistaken for Muhyiddin Ibn Arabi. In fact, he is often referred to as Al-Arabi, while Muhyiddin is referred to as Arabi.

[73] Ibn Khaldun, *Al-Muqaddimah*.

consider the fact that defying the Islamic leader of the society is only prohibited when the leader is a just one. In other words, it is religiously illegal to confront a just Islamic leader. And was there anyone more just and more rightful than Hussain to be the leader at that period of time?

Part 10

The Ninth Introduction: The Most Fundamental Factor Leading to the Occurrence of This Amazing Event: The Profound Faith and Love Imam Hussain (PBUH) Had for Islam, the Most Logical, the Clearest of Human Religions, the Religion in which Defending Human Life and Its Honor and Divine Dignity Is Seen as One of the Most Important Principles

As we discussed in the previous chapter, Islam and the finest of human virtues had been instilled deep within Imam Hussain's spirit from both external and internal sources. Having found out the ultimate answers to every major question a conscious, reasonable human being may have regarding the four main relationships (a human being's relationship with his own self, with Allah, with the universe and with other human beings), he had discovered how his existence within the main rhythm of the universe was. In other words, by means of finding the answers to the six fundamental questions – Who am I? Where have I come from? Where am I? Who am I with? Why have I come here? Where do I go from here?[74] – he had understood and lived in accordance with the truth about human life and its values in all aspects about "what there is" and "what there should be."

If such a great man – who had found the answers to the most comprehensive and basic questions about life – cannot discover the truth about life (and not just a few limited phenomena about life), definitely no one else will be able to do so, either. Imam Hussain's words (in particular his prayers) – which point out the finest kind of relationship with Allah, the universe as well as how human life should be – and also Imam Hussain's conduct from the time the Holy Prophet (PBUH) was alive up to the last moments of his life in the bloody plain of Nainawa clearly prove this.

---

[74] Although the four relationships and the six questions seem different, a carefully study of them will show the unity they in fact have. A human being's relationship with his own self, for instance, is included in two of the questions – "Who am I?" and "Why have I come here?" As for man's relationship with Allah, "Where have I come from?" and "Where do I go from here?" and "Why have I come here?" can be considered. "Where am I?" indicates man's relationship with the universe, and "Who am I with?" implies man's relationship with other human beings.

Now, as the tenth and last introduction to this book, we shall examine and interpret the factors influential in the sacrifices made by Imam Hussain (PBUH) and the roots which led to his martyrdom.

Part 11

The Tenth Introduction: What the Humanities Expects Scholars of Various Sects of Islam in the First Place and then Other Thinkers of Divine and Human Religions to Do regarding Careful Attention to the Unique Sacrifice Made by Imam Hussain (PBUH) to Save Human Values – Even Though Professionals in These Sciences May Neglect Such a Valuable Expectations!

We do not mean to imply that no work has been produced regarding Imam Hussain's astounding sacrifice to save human virtues. Due to the crucial significance of this issue, which is as vital as the importance of human virtues themselves, more research might have been done, for this unique event – which has countless aspects worthy of study – will last as long as man and mankind continue to exist.

This does not convey that Islamic books on history have neglected this issue, for all Islamic historians – and also some Western scholars studying the East – have researched the Karbala event and analyzed it to some extent. Nevertheless, this event is of such high significance that historians should have analyzed all aspects of it honestly and impartially without being influenced by their particular feelings so that their work could be judged by truth-seeking human beings.[75] Moreover, thinkers with analytical, critical minds who are familiar with the various aspects of physical and spiritual human life should – if they feel obliged to progress along the path of human evolution – present a detailed interpretation and analysis of this amazing event along with comprehensive explanations about the virtues and values

---

[75] The delusion may arise that no matter how hard historians may try to provide accounts of history without being influenced by their beliefs and principles, they will not be able to totally ignore what they firmly believe in. We have already explained this when discussing the third factor influential in our gaining correct knowledge and judgment of any major historical event motivated and caused by human virtues. The response to such a delusion is, as previously explained, that it is wrong for a historian to allow his faith in a person or a subject to influence and interfere with the definite facts or factors regarding the event, for each event occurring in the universe has its own natural form and relevant factors which must be accounted for in history with total honesty. Such caution is in no conflict, however, with the profound analyses, interpretations and reason-seeking which are necessary if one is to fully comprehend and get results from a historical event, particularly like that of Karbala.

(and also the anti-virtues) involved. Such a divine sense of duty can be found in dignified, honorable historians who really understand this great being called human rather than any writer who pretends to be a thinker and an anthropologist but in fact creates nothing more than caricatures of fake descriptions of mankind, thus spending his few days in this world showing off his knowledge!

There are two reasons why historians and researchers regarded as authorities in Shi'ism take the study of the Nainawa event quite seriously:

1. Shiites regard Hussain, the son of Ali, as their third Imam, a man endowed with all advantages and virtues a complete human being needs. They believe all of his deeds, words, and every aspect of his behavior to have been pure and faultless. This belief arises out of not only the life story of this great martyr of human virtues but also records and documents available regarding the lives of the Holy Prophet, Imam Ali, Fatima and Imam Hassan Mujtaba (Peace Be Upon Them) as well as other infallible Imams.

2. The same factors that have made Shiites[76] feel such passion for Ali ibn Abi Talib are also applicable to Imam Hussain (PBUH). Jibran Khalil Jibran[77] has thus described a few of these factors:

> *I believe that Ali, the son of Abi Talib, was the first Arab to be able to make contact with the basic soul and spirit of the whole universe. From him, people heard words they had never heard before. The stark contrast between the ignorance, decadence and darkness people had lived in previously, and his ways of eloquence had people astounded. Some were fascinated by his methods; their fascination was natural and essential. Those who opposed his styles of eloquence, however, were children of ignorance.*
>
> *Ali, the son of Abi Talib, died as a martyr of his own greatness. When he died, he was uttering words of prayer. He left this world with enthusiasm to meet his Allah. Arabs did not discover the truth about this great man until men from our Persian neighbors, those who could tell gems from pebbles, gave Ali's character some of the appreciation and recognition he deserved.*
>
> *He rushed toward eternity before he had the chance to fulfill the mission he had regarding human beings in the world. Nonetheless, I can visualize him with a smile on his face at the time he was dying.*
>
> *Ali, the son of Abi Talib, left this world for the eternal world, just like Allah-sent prophets who were appointed to cities which did not*

[76] Among Shiites of the world, the people of Iran have made a highly significant contribution – both qualitatively and quantitatively – when it comes to enthusiastic passion for the Holy Prophet and his progeny. Of course, this does not mean that Shi'ism and love for the Holy Prophet's family Is confined to Iran.

[77] Jibran Khalil Jibran (1883-1931) was a Lebanese-American poet, author and artist. [Translator]

deserve them, met people who did not deserve them, at a time which did not seem to be an appropriate era. However, your Allah has secrets only He is aware of.[78]

George Jordaq[79] then quotes the following views from Jibran Khalil Jibran:

Thus, Jibran sees Imam Ali as a prophet appointed to people who did not appreciate him, in a land which did not deserve him and at a time which was not right. From Jibran's point of view, Ali is a man of wisdom far superior to all wise men of all times. The Arabs lived in the rays of his goodness, but it was the Persians who made some progress thanks to his light. It took the Arab race ages to gradually be guided toward his ways of eloquence and the greatness of his character. Nonetheless, Ali, the son of Abi Talib, lived in the temple of absolute thought and spirit. He would only retreat into his own essence and nature when he wanted to provide human beings with words of eternal wisdom. Indeed, he was connected to springs of pure mystical knowledge.[80]

The well-known statement below is what Mu'awiyah told his son Yazid in order to warn him against engaging in any conflict or animosity toward Imam Hussain (PBUH):

Hussain is a man who carries in him the spirit of his father, Ali ibn Abi Talib.[81]

As reported by the late Muhaddith Qumi[82], the above statement is what Umar ibn Sa'ad quoted from Mu'awiyah to Shimr ibn Thiljawshan on the day before Ashura. As we have already mentioned, authorities and researchers from – both Muslim and non-Muslim – countries have also produced many books on the character of Imam Hussain (PBUH) and his amazing story, and it would be important and appropriate to collect them. Nevertheless, given the many virtues involved in this great movement and also the many anti-virtues displayed by Imam Hussain's adversaries (indeed, the most shameful kinds of wickedness can be witnessed in this event), there are still plentiful truths which remain untold and unsolved about Imam Hussain and his movement which calls for further study and research and will definitely prove to be useful for human evolution and development.

When a man with a great character like Hussain, the son of Ali, faces martyrdom, a motive as immense as making the aim of creating a reality is

---

[78] Jordaq, George, *Sautu'l Adalati'l Insaniyah ("Ali: The Voice of Human Justice")*.
[79] George Jordaq (1931-2014) was a Christian author and poet from Lebanon. [Translator]
[80] Jordaq, George, *Sautu'l Adalati'l Insaniyah ("Ali: The Voice of Human Justice")*
[81] Qumi, Shaikh Abbas (also known as Muhaddith Qumi), *Nafas ul-Mahmum*.
[82] Abbas Qumi (1877-1940), also known as Muhaddith Qumi, was a Shia scholar, historian, and *hadith* narrator. [Translator]

required. In this book, we shall attempt to study the character of Hussain as well as his martyrdom, his incentive, and its consequences. As the most obvious aspect of the astounding tale of Nainawa, we must first accept that when such a great man accepts martyrdom, and in such an appalling, bitter fashion, the incentive can be neither achieving wealth nor fame or power. It was not an act of personal vengeance, either. This is a fact no honest historian or authority can ever deny. Therefore, the only motive such a martyrdom may have would be to defend and revive Islam. It is thus scientifically necessary for us to briefly go over the identity and history of Islam before examining the context of the unique event of Karbala.

About 14 centuries ago, the greatest human-divine revolution in the history of mankind emerged by means of the power of divine revelations and miracles as well as the sincerest and diligent efforts of Muhammad (PBUH), the son of Abdullah and the last of the prophets.

Through the religion it provided mankind with, this revolution announced the culture of the originality of the finest of human virtues, equality, and brotherhood among all human beings and proved that they could be understood and made a reality. The religion brought about by this revolution is eternal due to the following two reasons:

1. The beliefs, laws, and decrees presented by Islam are connected to fixed human truths and man's basic needs as seen in the four relationships:
    - man's relationship with his own self,
    - man's relationship with Allah,
    - man's relationship with the universe, and
    - man's relationship with his fellow human beings.

It is only through such connection that man can find the answers to his most serious and most fundamental questions:
    - Who am I?
    - Where have I come from?
    - Where am I?
    - Who am I with?
    - Why have I come here?
    - Where do I go from here?

2. The excellent, constructive results man has attained by means of putting Islam to practical use, such as scientific and industrial advances, different worldviews, constructive mysticism and moral ethics – all of which have, as admitted by fair researchers both in the East and in the West, brought about amazing evolutionary impact in the world.

Another highly important advantage was that this new religion presented the main context of Abraham's religion to the world once again. We shall now present a very brief list of examples of studies done regarding the achievements mentioned above by Western and Eastern researchers. Obviously, had we intended to provide a rather more comprehensive list of such works of research, a group of scientists and thinkers would definitely have been required in order to collaborate and compile a large encyclopedia which could fill dozens of volumes.

Here is a concise list of sources which can serve as but an example of Eastern and Western studies on the consequences brought about by the emergence of Islam:

1. *Allahs Sonne über dem Abendland" ("Allah's Sun over the Occident")* by Dr. Sigrid Hunke.
2. *Islamic Surveys: The Influence of Islam on Medieval Europe,* by W. Montgomery Watt.
3. *Science and Religion in Intelligible Life,* by Muhammad Taqi Jafari.
4. *A History of Science,* by George Sarton.
5. *La Civilisation des Arabes* (1884), later published in English as *The World of Islamic Civilization* (1974).
6. Tarikh al-Tamaddun al-Islami ("History of Islamic Civilization"), by Jurji Zaydan.
7. *A Post-Islam History of Medicine in Iran,* by Dr. Mahmoud Najmabadi (originally in Persian).
8. *Science in Islam,* by Ahmad Aram (originally in Persian).
9. *La science Arabe et son rôle dans l'évolution Scientifique Mondiale,* by Aldo Mieli.
10. *Histoire de la Science, by Pierre Rousseau.*
11. *Sources on the History of Islamic Sciences, by Sayyid Hussain Nasr.*
12. *Science in History,* by John D. Bernal.
13. *Introduction to the History of Science. Volume I, from Homer to Umar Khayyam, and Volume II, from Rabbi Ben Ezra to Roger Bacon,* by George Sarton.
14. *Storia dell'astronomia presso gli Arabi Nel Medioevo Evo,* by Carlo Alfonso Nallino.
15. *The Historical Background of Chemistry,* by Henry Marshall Leicester.
16. *How Greek science passed to the Arabs,* by De Lacy O'Leary.
17. *The Philosopher of Rey (Muhammad ibn Zakariyya Razi),* supervised by Dr. Mehdi Muhaqqiq.
18. *Philosophy Since Earliest History,* Vols. 3-4 and 5-6, by Muhammad Rashad (originally in Arabic).
19. *A'lam ul-Falsafat ul-Arabiyyah,* Kamal Yazaju and Antoun Qattash Karam (originally in Arabic).
20. *Dirasat fi Tarikh ul-Arabiyyat ul-Islamiyyah,* by Abduh Al-Shumali (originally in Arabic).
21. *Tarikh ul-Hukama,* by Ali ibn Yusuf Qafti (originally in Arabic).
22. *Selected Works from Iranian Divine Philosophers,* by Sayyid Jalaluddin Ashtiani and Henri Corbin (in 4 volumes).
23. *A History of Muslim Philosophy (Vols. 1 and 2),* by M. M. Sharif.
24. *Nuzhat al arwâh wa rawhat al-afrâh,* by Shams al-Din Muhammad ibn Mahmud Shahrazuri.

25. *A History of Great Islamic Universities*, by Abdul Rahim Qanimat.
26. *The Story of Civilization*, by Will Durant, *The Age of Faith*.
27. *A Popular History*, Vol. 5, by John Hammerton.
28. *Dirasat wa Buhuth fil Tarikh wal Islam*, Jafar Murtadh Al-Amili (originally in Arabic).
29. *A Study of History*, by Arnold J. Toynbee.
30. *Tarikh ul-Bimaristanat fi Islam*, by Dr. Ahmad Isa Bek (originally in Arabic).
31. *Al-Thaqafat ul-Islamiyyah wa l-Hayat ul-Mu'asirah*, by Muhammad Khalafullah.
32. *How Iran and Islam Have Served One Another*, by the Martyred Scholar Murtaza Mutahhari.
33. *Al-Mujtami' ul-Islami*, by Allamah Muhammad Taqi Mudarrisi.
34. *L'islam: impressions et études*, by Henri Marie de La Croix Castries, comte de.
35. *Al-fikr ul-Islami*, by Allamah Sayyid Muhammad Taqi Mudarresi (originally in Arabic).
36. *Islam's Contribution to the World's Civilization*, by Dr. Sahibuzzamani.
37. *Al-Islam Yaqud al-Hayah ("Islam Leads the Life")*, by Sayyid Muhammad Baqir Sadr (originally in Arabic).
38. *Al-Muqaddimah*, by Ibn Khaldun.
39. *Al-watha'iq us-Siyasiyyah*, by Dr. Muhammad Hamidullah.
40. *The New World of Islam*, by Theodore Lothrop Stoddard.
41. *The Portfolio of Islam*, by Dr. Zarrinkoub.
42. *Al-Islam wal Hadharatul Arabiyyah*, by Muhammad Kurd Ali (originally in Arabic).
43. *Die Renaissance des Islams*, by Adam Mez.
44. *A Political History of Islam*, by Hassan Bana (3 volumes).
45. *Ma'alim ul-Qurbah fi Ahkam ul-Husbah*, by Ibn Al-Ikhwah Damishqi.
46. *Al-Fikr ul-Islami wat Tatawur*, by Fathi Uthman (originally in Arabic).
47. *The Political Philosophy of Islam*, by Abulfazl Ezzati (originally in Persian).
48. *The Fundamentals of Relations and Correspondences in Islamic Management*, by Sayyid Mahmoud Syahpoush (originally in Persian).
49. *The Biography of Umar ibn Abdul Aziz*, by Malik ibn Anas (originally in Arabic).
50. *Political Thoughts of Contemporary Islam*, by Hamid Enayat.
51. *Al-Islam wa Mantiq ul-Quwwah*, by Sayyid Muhammad Hussain Fadhlullah.

The story of how Imam Hussain's Islamic revolution emerged and progressed has been penned by well-trusted historians, and those enthusiastic, sincere human beings interested can gain enough information about this story from the books available. The most important thing that a historian of profound insight is attracted to when studying the identity of this religious revolution and how it arose is a characteristic about it which is unprecedented: there are no cultural, military, legal, ethical, economic or religious backgrounds required for such a revolution. A careful study of the grounds which led to previous movements and revolutions indicates how significant this point is. All previous revolutions had been provided with the factors and conditions needed for them to occur. Let us see what Muhammad Iqbal Lahori[83]'s views are:

> Regarding original unity among human beings, the Quran has said [Women 4:1] that 'Your Lord has created all of you from one single person', but imagining life in the form of a well-established, general unity is something that will take time, and nations will have to become involved in the main context of global events in order to develop. Rapidly spreading into a great empire, Islam had brought mankind the message of equality. [It is to be noted that it would be unimaginable for even the largest empire to preach equality if the importance of equality had not been included in the ideology of Islam already.] Christian Rome, on the other hand, was not able to perceive such an image of mankind. As Flint[84] rightly says, 'No Christian writer – and no other writer in the Roman Empire – can be found who has gone any further than general, abstract principles of human unity.'[85]

Muhammad Iqbal Lahori has also quoted from a historian on civilizations:

> It seemed that the civilization which had taken four thousand years to build was about to fall apart, and that mankind was prone to be thrown back into darkness, ignorance, and barbarianism… The writer then adds that the world was in need of a new culture which could replace despotic power and breathe in new unity instead of unity based on blood bonds. He states that it is surprising that the culture so badly needed arose out of the Arabian Peninsula.[86]

This surprise can be alleviated by man's noting that a supernatural factor, a metaphysical agent beyond human thoughts and perceptions, is needed in order to establish true unity (and not a fake, imaginary one or a unity brought about by whimsical desires or compulsion), and divine instructions have not specified a particular position or location where this factor – which can found a true civilization – should be activated.

> **O mankind! Have reverence your Lord, Who created you from a single person.**[87]

---

[83] Allamah Muhammad Iqbal (1877-1938) was a Muslim philosopher and poet from Pakistan. [Translator]

[84] Scottish philosopher Robert Flint (1838–1910). [Translator]

[85] Iqbal, Muhammad (1930): *The Reconstruction of Religious Thought in Islam.*

[86] Ibid.

[87] Women (4:1).

*   *   *

It is He Who hath produced you from a single person.[88]

Moreover, another verse of the Holy Quran (The Table Spread 5:32) has implied that unity among the whole of mankind is to be regarded as being superior to all qualities, quantities, and aspects of natural life.

To demonstrate that the main unity of mankind has been depicted quite firmly and explicitly in the major context of the basic source of Islam, we shall discuss twelve kinds of equalities and three kinds of unities in the next chapter.

Before engaging in that discussion, however, there is an important point to be noted: **Islam's call for equality and unity among human beings is so important that even if Islam had no other reason with which to establish divine essence, eternity and comprehensiveness, the call for equality and unity would suffice.**

---

[88] The Cattle (6:98).

Part 12

Equalities and Unities

We need to begin by discussing what "equality" and "unity" mean.

Equality

It is needless to say that equality in this context does not refer to a complete similarity or homogeneity between human individuals. By the same token, it does not mean that human individuals have the same characteristics, since it is basically a false impression of reality and even no two inanimate things would be similar in such way, let alone animals or human beings who are the most complicated creatures on the planet when it comes to free will and numerous capacities, forces and possibilities. Thus, human differences are not merely accidental phenomena, but rather genuine in the sense that they are essential prerequisites of human existence, as it is reflected in the general principle: *As long as a thing has not been individuated by its individual characteristics, it could not exist.*

Then what do fraternity and equality mean in this context? To explain this issue, we need to mention that equality here does not refer to a comprehensive issue in all human respects, but rather three equalities in relation to each other:

1. Equality in relation to the supreme source and principles of existence.
2. Equality in the essence and essential qualities.
3. Covenantal equality before natural and positive laws and other rules, which are necessary for the regulation of natural and intelligible life.

These three equalities are divided into twelve principal kinds. Human unities, which are above the equalities, can be categorized into three major kinds. We shall now discuss them here.

The natural equality of human beings can be divided into two kinds:

1. Physical similarity and homogeneity, which is also visible even in other natural bodies; nevertheless, the similarity in this respect could not be a thorough homogeneity. As Rumi says in Book 2 of his *Mathnawi*:

> *Incomplete examples and similes serve to relieve man of his confusion and awe;*
> *for indeed, no two beings in this world are the same.*

Moreover, this has also eloquently been depicted in the following mystic rule:

> *No repetition is possible in physical manifestations of deity.*

2. Equality in intangible truths like intellection, imagination, wills, associations of concepts, pleasures, pains and so on and so forth. This is a higher equality than physical equality, as the intangible is essentially more valuable. Therefore, there is truth within human beings that, it perceived, can also lead to the perception of them in others as well.

Unity

Unity in this context does not refer to an absolute unity that could not be manifested but in a supra-quantitative one; rather, it consists of the state of the union in a reality that human individuals can conceive themselves as the parts of the same reality. Thus conceived, human individuals are the closely interwoven constitutive parts of a whole. This shared reality, which represents a whole, can be divided into three kinds:

I.   A reality that is like a whole – but not a genuine whole – that is the total sum of its parts, such as a society.

II. The similarity that unites all human individuals with each other like the waves of the same sea. The following verses of the Holy Quran (The Table Spread 5:32) indicate this unity:

> *For this reason did We prescribe to the children of Israel that whoever slays a soul, unless it be for manslaughter or mischief in the land, it is as though he slew all men; and whoever keeps it alive, it is as though he kept alive all men; and certainly Our messengers came to them with clear arguments, but even after that many of them certainly act extravagantly in the land.*

Another verse depicting this kind of unity is as follows (The Cattle 6:98):

> *And He it is Who has brought you into being from a single soul, then there is (for you) a resting-place and a depository; indeed, We have made plain the communications for people who understand.*

III. The acquired unity that could be achieved through acting upon the moral principles and self-purification of evils and carnal passions. This, in fact, is the time when human beings can understand the pleasures and pains felt by each other and experience the divine state of the union.

Thus, human similarities are of two kinds:

1) Equalities and

2) Unities.

Unities can be categorized into three groups:
1. Unity in the sense of parts of an arbitrary whole, such as the human society that is consisted of real individuals.
2. A unity above all natural unities and multiplicities, which is not acquired.
3. Unity based on acquired dignity, which exposes human individuals to the eternal sparks of divine majesty.

The Twelve-fold Equalities

The unities and equalities discussed here have been driven from authentic Islamic texts; not only do they demonstrate that the idea of human rights has its roots in Islam, but they also show that the universal idea of human rights presumes human evolutionary movement. There are numerous indications in human sciences and cultures about the unity that can be taken as the basis for a just and peaceful coexistence. But no other school of thought has addressed this serious issue better than Islam. According to Islam, there are twelve kinds of equalities and three kinds of unities between human beings:[89]

The First Kind: Equality in Relation to the Creator

All human beings have been created by a transcendental being who is the Creator of all creatures, as depicted in the following verse of the Holy Quran:

> *Allah is He who created you, then gave you sustenance, then He causes you to die, then brings you to life. Is there any of your associate-Allah who does aught of it? Glory be to Him, and exalted be He above what they associate (with Him).*[90]

The existence of the Divine Being has already been demonstrated by several reasons and His being the Creator of all creatures is a self-evident reality. By understanding this equality, all human individuals could recognize that they all are equally subjected to Divine Love unless they have deprived themselves of this divine bounty by committing evil acts.

---

[89] Some thinkers suffice to the indication of the indispensability of equality and unity and thus do not give any indication of its reasons and kinds. In his magnum opus *De L' Esprit de Lois*, Montesquieu has stated, "Human rights are civil laws of the world; that is to say, as in every country the citizens enjoy their civil laws, in the world every nation shall enjoy universal human rights, and before these rights every nation is like an individual in the human society." Nonetheless, the revealed religions can only meaningfully address the issue of universal equalities and unities of human beings and have the claim for a global family of human beings.

[90] The Romans (30:40).

The Second Kind: Equality in the Wisdom of the Ultimate Goal

We mean here the Divine Wisdom that has created human individuals and put them in the course of ultimate goal they are equally equipped to reach using making sincere efforts. The divine wisdom that has rendered the creation of human beings in this world possible consists of illuminative domination of "the human self" over the world through being exposed to

absolute perfection which could lead a human being to *Visio Dei* by sincere efforts in the course of intelligible life. This is the true meaning of Divine Service that has been described as the philosophy of the creation of jinn and man in the Holy Quran (The Scatterers 51:56):

> *And I have not created jinn and man except that they should serve me.*

The Third Kind: Equality in Human Beings' Deserving to Have the Divine Spirit Breathed into All of Them

> *Then He made him complete and breathed into him of His spirit, and made for you the ears and the eyes and the hearts; little is it that you give thanks.*[91]

The Fourth Kind: Equality in the Planting of the Seeds of Divine Knowledge within Man

> *And He taught Adam all the names, then presented them to the angels; then He said: Tell me the names of those if you are right.*[92]

This verse has surely been revealed as a response from Allah to the angels regarding the creation of Adam and his children rather than Adam himself, for the question asked by the angels did not pertain to the creation of Adam himself, for he had not shed blood; it was about Adam's children, who had each other's blood on their hands.

The Fifth Kind: Equality in the Factor of the Perfection Which Forms the Context of the Divine Message

It is needless to say that all true religions have been revealed for humanity by the Lord, and regarding their primordial unity, the Divine Message of revealed religions is one – and it is Abraham's Religion:

> *The messenger believes in what has been revealed to him from his Lord, and (so do) the believers; they all believe in Allah and his angels and his books and his messengers; we make*

---

[91] Adoration (32:9).
[92] The Cow (2:31).

no difference between any of his messengers; and they say: we hear and obey, our lord! Thy forgiveness (do we crave), and to Thee is the eventual course.[93]

*   *   *

He has made plain to you of the religion what he enjoined upon Noah, and that which we have revealed to you and that which we enjoined upon Abraham and Moses and Jesus that keep to obedience and be not divided therein; hard to the unbelievers is that which you call them to; Allah chooses for himself whom he pleases, and guides to himself him who turns (to him), frequently.[94]

It is a demonstrable reality that the Holy Quran has revealed Abraham's message without any distortion.

The Sixth Kind: Equality in the Inherent Dignity (i.e., the Highest Dignity) Allah Has Blessed All Human Beings With

And surely, We have honored the children of Adam, and We carry them in the land and the sea, and We have given them of the good things, and We have made them excel by an appropriate excellence over most of those whom We have created.[95]

The Seventh Kind: Equality in the Potential to Achieve and Use Acquired Dignity

O, you men! Surely, we have created you of a male and a female, and made you tribes and families that you may know each other; surely the most honorable of you with Allah is the one among you most careful (of his duty); surely Allah is knowing, aware.[96]

The Eighth Kind: Equality in General Orientation

The goals that human beings seek in their life are either related with their natural life or related with their ideal life; moreover, both forms of life are oriented by a primordial sense of self-preservation.

---

[93] The Cow (2:285).
[94] The Counsel (42:13).
[95] The Children of Israel (17:70).
[96] The Apartments (49:13).

The Ninth Kind: Equality in the Origin of Creation of Human Beings

All human beings have been created from one spirit. As the Holy Quran has stated (Women 4:1):

> *O, people! Be careful of (your duty to) your lord, who created you from a single being and created its mate of the same (kind) and spread from these two, many men and women; and be careful of (your duty to) Allah, by whom you demand one of another (your rights), and (to) the ties of relationship; surely Allah ever watches over you.*

Sa'adi has eloquently poeticized these equalities (the eighth and ninth forms) in the following renowned lines of his poetry:

> *Human beings are members of a whole,*
> *in the creation of one essence and soul.*
> *If one member is afflicted with pain,*
> *other members uneasy will remain.*
> *If you've no sympathy for human pain,*
> *the name "human" you cannot retain!*

In his *Divan-e Shams*, Rumi, on the other hand, gives a deeper account of this transcendent equality of humanity:

> *What is all of this uproar, drunken craziness and conflict in aid of?*
> *Are we all not members of the same group following the same path?!*

In his *Mathnawi*, Rumi has also written:

> *If you see great men of Allah together,*
> *even if there may be hundreds of thousands of them,*
> *do not think that they are arrogant or wrongdoing;*
> *in fact, they are all like one, like an ocean of water,*
> *their large numbers like the waves of the ocean.*
> *To the simple mind, this will seem like multiplicity,*
> *whereas it is nothing but unity indeed.*
> *One who is aware of what water and wind are like,*
> *knows only too well that these plentiful waves are caused by the wind upon the sea,*
> *and will never contradict the unity of the ocean.*
> *Have you not seen sunlight passing through many different holes at the same time?*
> *Does that imply that the sunlight is not one but many? By no means!*
> *Likewise, men of Allah have each contained the Holy Divine Spirit within themselves; indeed, those who feel doubtful about this are in fact captive of the layers of their own physical being.*
> *Such divisions and multiplicities exist in fact only in animal spirits; human spirits, on the other hand, are one.*[97]

---

[97] Rumi's *Mathnawi*, Book 2.

The Tenth Kind: Equality in the Main Matter of Creation

There are several verses in the Holy Quran that introduce the earth as the matter of human creation:

> *And certainly We created man of clay that gives forth sound, of black mud fashioned in shape.*[98]

The Lord has commissioned the sperm undergoing development within mothers' wombs to sustain human generations:

> *He created man from a small seed.*[99]

The Eleventh Kind: Equality in Human Essence – the Nature and Qualities All Human Beings Possess

All human individuals have different physical and mental peculiarities. That is to say, although all human individuals have been created from a single spirit breathed by the Lord into them all; nonetheless, they enjoy different physical and mental peculiarities that make their individuality. However, Allah the Almighty has reminded His servants of these shared realities. We shall now cite three verses of the Holy Quran which indicate these shared realities:

1. The fact that all human beings are equal in their being endowed with the Divine Spirit has been pointed in The Rock (15:29) and Saad (38:72):

    > *So, when I have proportioned him and breathed into him of My [created] soul, then fall down to him in prostration.*

2. There are at least forty verses in the Holy Quran that directly refer to human reason:

    > *Already have We shown the Signs plainly to you, that ye may learn wisdom.*[100]

3. A few examples of Quranic verses regarding conscience are:

    > *Though he puts forth his excuses, do not move your tongue with it to make haste with it.*[101]

    *   *   *

    > *Nay! I swear by the self-accusing soul.*[102]

    *   *   *

---

[98] The Rock (15:26).
[99] The Bee (16:4).
[100] The Iron (57:17).
[101] The Resurrection (75:14-15).
[102] The Resurrection (75:2).

The Twelfth Kind: Equality in Laws

The Three Kinds of Unities

The First Kind: The Unity beyond All Unities and Differences

This unity exclusively belongs to revealed religions alone. As Allah Almighty has stated in the Holy Quran (The Table Spread 5:32):

> *For this reason, did We prescribe to the children of Israel that whoever slays a soul, unless it be for manslaughter or for mischief in the land, it is as though he slew all men; and whoever keeps it alive, it is as though he kept alive all men; and certainly our messengers came to them with clear arguments, but even after that many of them certainly act extravagantly in the land.*

There are two points in this verse that are worth to be noted:

1. This holy verse could be summarized in a mathematical formula: all=1 and 1=all. This is the true remedy of all human pains.
2. This unity is a supra-natural reality that could be used as the basis of all universal rights for humanity.

The Second Kind of Unity: Unity by Acquired Dignity Existing between Spiritually Matured Human Beings

> *The believers are but brethren, therefore make peace between your brethren and be careful of (your duty to) Allah that mercy may be had on you.*[103]

> *   *   *

> *Surely (as for) those who believe and do good deeds for them will Allah bring about love.*[104]

Moreover, Abu Basir has quoted Imam Al-Sadiq (PBUH) as saying:

> *The believer is the brother of his fellow believers like the organs of the same body; if one organ is afflicted with pain, he feels the pain of that organ. The spirits of believers come from the same Divine Spirit, and the connection between the believer's spirit and Allah's Spirit is even stronger than the connection between the sun and its rays.*[105]

This form of unity is the highest of all unities, since it originates from the divine attraction between enlightened spirits. This unity is acquired and is thus more valuable on account of the efforts which should be made by human individuals.

---

[103] The Apartments (49:10).

[104] Mary (19:96).

[105] Al-Kulayni, *Usul al-Kafi*, Vol. 2.

The Third Kind of Unity: Social Unity

All human individuals together form the society and the whole constitution of the society is dependent upon all human individuals. Thus conceived, the individuals' destinies are interwoven. In other words, in this kind of unity, the specifications of the whole society affect the fundamental features and proneness to causes of every member of the society. Thus, the good or evil they experience is totally intertwined. The Holy Prophet Muhammad (Peace Be upon Him) has been quoted as saying:

> *A group of people got on a ship and everyone took his own seat. One of them started to make a hole in his seat. "What are you doing?" the other passengers asked. "It is my own seat and I am boring into my own place." If the passengers try to stop him, they could save their lives and the ship; otherwise, they are all doomed to death.*[106]

It is thanks to these equalities and unities as seen by Islam that led to the emergence of true human unity (and not a unity based on hallucination, imagination, compulsion or whimsical emotion, cases of which are plentiful throughout history in various societies and nations) in the desert lands of the Arabian Peninsula.

---

[106] From Reza Mobasheri's translation of Thomas Paine's *Rights of Man*.

Part 13

Having Devoted Himself to His Mission and Selflessly Attempting to Perfect the Religion He Presented Mankind with, the Holy Prophet (PBUH) Passed Away

Muhammad Mustapha (PBUH), the Holy Prophet of Islam, Allah's last chosen as prophet, having succeeded – thanks to Allah's kindness – within a limited period of time in achieving accomplishing his mission of preaching human evolution, passed away.

For many years after the decease of the shining sun of Islam – about half a century – the world witnessed the most complex events in the history of mankind. The reason why such complicated and at times contradictory events occurred lies in the fact that politics – the management of the ordinary aspects about people – at the hand of some of those in charge cast vagueness upon the Holy Quran's clear order stating that everyone should "obey Allah and obey His prophet" (Women 4:59), and an unjustified concept of *ijtihad* (independent reasoning or the utmost effort an individual can put forth in an activity) found itself confronting Allah's revelations!

In that critical period of history, although there still were some who were faithful and loyal lovers of Islam, a group of wealth-greedy, evil, domineering men rose to power and the grounds cultivated by the Holy Prophet (PBUH) and his family and companions to be an arena for people to compete in good and perfection along the path of a global civilization for all of mankind were in fact turned into a place for them to fulfill their own selfish ambitions.

As the conscious and wise members of the society expected, the evil desires and wishes that those opportunists had suppressed within themselves ever since the decadent, ignorant days before Islam arose once again and intensely gusted through the whole, newly-formed Islamic community. The concept of divine caliphate, which had originated and flourished long a divine, righteous path, now vanished from the horizon of the society due to those whimsical, worldly desires.

Divine evolution cannot be realized through force and compulsion; that is why no human movement or revolution has been able to provide an effective weapon to eradicate the roots of deviation which have long existed in the hearts of the people of some societies.

Thus, it is no surprise for a man known as Mu'awiyah from the Umayyids to rise out of the Islamic community and put up intense resistance against Ali, the son of Abi Talib, a man who ruled based on the most original and the clearest of sources of law.

At that time, Mu'awiyah – quite wrongfully – rose to seek vengeance for Uthman's blood [a claim that, if rightful, would have called for Mu'awiyah to take legal action rather than show himself as deserving to rule the vast Islamic society] and thus confronted the righteous ruler Ali!

Overcome by the storm of greed and lust for racist domineering, Mu'awiyah brazenly wreaked havoc among the progress the Muslims were making, thus bringing the Islamic movement to a halt. There is no doubt that ordinary conquests and expanding the Islamic territory had not been the original intention of the man who founded true Islam. In fact, as the conduct of the Holy Prophet (PBUH) shows, his aim was to further the cause of human evolution.

Part 14

Who Was Mu'awiyah? What Did He Do?

Historians, Khair al-Din al-Zarkali for instance, have written that:

> Mu'awiyah, the son of Abu Sufyan and the father of Yazid, was appointed as the governor of Jordan during the reign of Umar ibn al-Khattab. Then, after the death of his brother Yazid, the son of Abu Sufyan, Umar appointed him to govern Damascus. During the reign of Uthman, the son of Affan, he took over the whole of Syria.[107]

There is a question that needs to be answered here. After Uthman's death, Mu'awiyah became a man who would break or defy any law and commit any wrongdoing necessary to help him achieve his power-greedy goals; but why did that aspect of his character not reveal itself during the reigns of the two previous rulers? Why was his true character kept hidden? The only answer that could be to some extent convincing is the same point we have seen throughout the course of history regarding figures of Machiavellian characteristics; those who can behave – for a lifetime – in a way which is in contrast to their true personality. All historians agree that Mu'awiyah used Islam – a religion which aims to unite all races, communities and nations based on human unity – in order to further his own personal goal: to rise to power. As an attempt to transform the Islamic government into Arab dominance and shift power to his own clan, Mu'awiyah stopped at none, even if it meant using his sword to establish the rule of his son, one of the most wicked criminals history has seen. Historians have reported that whenever Umar ibn al-Khattab looked at Mu'awiyah, he said:

> Indeed, he is the Kasra [i.e. "the king"] of Arabs.[108]

> *   *   *

> It was during his era when coins were made carrying portraits of an Arab with a sword at his waist.[109]

When Ad-Dahak ibn Qays was giving a eulogy on Mu'awiyah after his death, one of the things he said to describe Mu'awiyah was, "Mu'awiyah was the

---

[107] Al-Zarkali, *Al-A'lam ("The Renowned")*, Vol. 8.
[108] Ibid. Also see Al-Suyuti's *Tarikh al-Khulafa*, and *Al-Bidayah*, Vol. 8, quoted in Abdul Razzaq al-Muqarram's *Maqtal al-Hussain*.
[109] Ibid.

safe haven for Arabs." Moreover, as Ibn Khaldun has written:

> *Then, as the nature of being the ruler necessitated, Mu'awiyah took measures to become more powerful and superior to others and dominate them. Such a way of governance was not appropriate for Mu'awiyah, but it was natural for his prejudice to make him act so. Furthermore, the Umayyad clan had the aggressive and brutal disposition required to behave that way.*[110]

In a highly renowned *hadith*, the Holy Prophet (PBUH) has implied that Mu'awiyah and his followers were oppressors and wrongdoers. As the Holy Prophet (PBUH) told Ammar:

> *O Ammar! You will be killed by a group of oppressive wrongdoers.*[111]

A disciple of Ali's, Ammar was eventually killed by Mu'awiyah's troops in the Siffin battles. Historians have also written:

> *When Uthman was under siege, he asked Mu'awiyah for help. Mu'awiyah dispatched no men, however. With the siege on Uthman intensifying, Mu'awiyah sent Yazid ibn Asad Qashiri. 'When you get to Zi Khashab [on the outskirts of Madina], stop. As an excuse, you can say that if you had been involved in the Uthman event, you would have seen things which would have obliged you to do something to help Uthman in my absence. So, do nothing, for I have helped.' Thus, Yazid ibn Asad stayed in Zi Khashab until Uthman was killed.*[112]

---

[110] Ibn Khaldun, *Muqaddameh Tarikh ("An Introduction to History")*.

111 This *hadith* has been quoted from Akramah by Al-Bukhari in his *Sahih al-Bukhari* as well as Ahmad ibn Hanbal in his *Musnad*. Moreover, Hafiz Jalaluddin Al-Suyuti has quoted the statement from various sources. See Al-Sayyid Muhammad al-Alawi al-Hussaini, *Al-Nasa'ih ul-Kafiyah liman Yatawalla Mu'awiyah*, and also Ibn Hisham's *Sira*, Vol. 2, and Al-Halabi, *Al-Sirat ul-Halabiyah*, Vol. 2.

[112] Ahmad ibn Yahya al-Baladhuri, *Ansab ul-Ashraf*, quoted from Muhammad al-Alawi's *Al-Nasai'h ul-Kafiyah*.

Then, this pioneer of Machiavellian ways of thinking[113] rose against Imam Ali (PBUH) in seek of vengeance for Uthman's blood, despite the fact that not only had Imam Ali (PBUH) played no role in Uthman's murder, but he had in fact taken serious measures in order to prevent it. Acting on such a baseless excuse, Mu'awiyah confronted Imam Ali (PBUH) in an ambitious effort to gain power during the few days he had in this world. Thus, under the façade of defending Islam, he in fact deprived mankind of the good Imam Ali (PBUH) was doing.

Since Mu'awiyah's styles of deception and guile and how he confronted righteousness and those who upheld good have been studied extensively, we shall here confine ourselves to Jalaliddin Al-Suyuti's point of view:

> *As Ibn Abi Shaiba has quoted from Sa'id bin Sa'id bin Jamhan: 'I told Safinah that the Umayyad clan believed that the caliphate belonged to them alone.' 'They are lying,' he replied. 'The Umayyads are the most vicious rulers of all, and Mu'awiyah is the first one.'*

---

[113] By saying that Mu'awiyah was a pioneer of Machiavellian ways of thinking, we mean that even before Machiavelli wrote his work *The Prince*, Mu'awiyah had put his advice to work – if a politician intends to do great things, he does not need to keep his promises and pledges. In fact, a politician needs to be as cunning as a wolf and as savagely vicious as a lion. [As all historians confirm, despite the heavy emphasis Islam has put upon keeping one's promises, Mu'awiyah quite ignorantly broke all of the promises and pledges he had made with Imam Hassan Mujtaba (PBUH)]. See Mustafavi, Sayyid Hussain, *Bismarck* (originally published in Persian).

Let us now consider examples of these two qualities in Mu'awiyah's conduct. Ibn Own has reported, "Sometimes people would tell Mu'awiyah, 'O Mu'awiyah! We swear to Allah that if you do not behave right, we shall put you right.' 'And how will you do that?' Mu'awiyah would ask. 'With a stick,' the people would reply. 'Well, in that case,' Mu'awiyah would say, 'very well, I shall behave right.' This is how cunningly deceptive and cool he was. As for his ruthless, vicious side, although he had strongly promised some of the most pious and most distinguished figures of the Islamic society (men such as Hujr ibn Adi, Sharik bin Shaddad Hazrami, Seifi ibn Fasil Shaibani, Qabisat ibn Sabi'a Abasi, Mihraz ibn Shahab Minqari, Kedam ibn Hayyan Anzi and Abdul Rahman ibn Hassan Anzi) that they would be granted immunity and safety, he killed them all in the most terrible way possible. (See Muhammad Al-Alawi, *Al-Nasa'ih ul-Kafiyah*)

As Al-Masudi has written, "Mu'awiyah had intrigued two Lakhmids to kill Abbas ibn Rabi'a Hashimi during the Siffin battles. Meanwhile, Amr ibn Al-As told Mu'awiyah, 'I know that Ali, the son of Abi Talib, is righteous, and we [me, you and our followers] are in conflict with good...'" (Ibid, as quoted from Al-Masudi's *Muruj-ul Thahab*)

As Amr ibn Al-As has explicitly confessed, the animosity Mu'awiyah began against Ali arose out of his ability to have many faces and be highly deceptive – a quality all Allah-sent religions have advised people to prevent.

> *Also, Salafi quoted from Abdullah ibn Ahmad ibn Hanbal, who said,*
> *'I once asked my father about Ali and Mu'awiyah. My father said*
> *that Ali had many enemies. No matter how hard his enemies tried*
> *to find a weakness or a fault in him, however, they failed. Therefore,*
> *they began over-praising his adversary, Mu'awiyah. That was the*
> *trick they devised.'*[114]

It is quite unlikely for someone with comprehensive and accurate knowledge of the school of thought of Islam and its divine philosophy, moral ethics and legal system who knows that the Holy Prophet of Islam intended to develop human beings of elevated, divine spirits to examine Mu'awiyah's character, his way of governance and what he did and not conclude that Mu'awiyah wreaked havoc in Islam and spread (albeit crude) Machiavellian theories in Islamic societies.

In response to the letter Muhammad ibn Abi Bakr had written from Egypt as an attempt to condemn Mu'awiyah for confronting Imam Ali (PBUH) and threaten and warn him against doing so, Mu'awiyah (this "inversed human being" as Imam Ali had described him) wrote:

> *I was there during the Prophet's reign, and so was your father. I*
> *knew that Ali ibn Abi Talib was better than me, and I had accepted*
> *that he was the righteous one. But when the Prophet received Allah's*
> *reward and completed his mission, your father and his Faruq [i.e.*
> *Umar] were the first ones to deprive Ali of what was rightfully*
> *his. They collaborated and opposed him. Had your father not done*
> *so, I would never have confronted Ali and would have handed the*
> *caliphate over to him.*[115]

In a cunning, Machiavellian-style strategy, Mu'awiyah thus puts the three former rulers in one group as collaborators in order to justify for Muhammad ibn Abi Bakr the campaign he had begun.

Having turned the spring and flourish Islam was enjoying into a fruitless autumn, Mu'awiyah usef a variety of deceptions and threats as well as sharp swords[116] to appoint his son Yazid – about whom no historian has ever had any doubt regarding his corruption and wrongdoing[117] – to rule the Islamic communities. As Abdul Rahman ibn Abi Bakr put it, "Indeed this was how the likes of Caesar and Heraclius did things."[118]

> *Al-A'amash*[119] *has reported that Amr bin Murrah quoted from Sa'id*

---

[114] Al-Suyuti, *Tarikh ul-Khulafa*.

[115] Nasr ibn Muzahim, *Waq'at Siffin ("The Battle of Siffin")*, Egypt. Also see Al-Masudi's *Muruj-ul Thahab*, Vol. 2, Egypt, Ibn Abi l-Hadid, *Sharh Nahjul Balaghah*, Vol. 1, and Ahmad Zaki Safwat, *Jamharat Rasa'il ul-Arab*, Vol. 1.

[116] Ibn Khaldun, *Al-Muqaddimah*. Also see Ahmad ibn Abi Yaqub, *Tarikh Yaqubi*, Vol. 2.

[117] Ibid.

[118] Al-Suyuti, *Tarikh ul-Khulafa*.

[119] Sulayman ibn Mahran al-Asadi al-A'amash, a scholar of *hadith*.

ibn Suwayd, who said that once, on a Friday, Mu'awiyah said the Friday prayers with us in Nukhilah, and during his sermon, he said, 'I swear to Allah that my battle against you was not to make you say prayers, fast, go to Haj and pay zakat. You do those things already. My war against you was for one purpose alone – to rule over you and dominate you. Allah has blessed me with this dominance and power, but you do not accept it.'[120]

In his above statements, which were delivered at a formal, public sermon, Mu'awiyah has confessed to three significant points:

1.   He did not engage in battle in order to propagate or save Islam, for the people of Iraq were already Muslims and observed the duties Islam expected them to fulfill. Even before someone could ask him why he was fighting them, he said that the purpose of his battle was to dominate and rule.

Mu'awiyah's words were so threatening and so intimidating, however, that no one dared to say, "We had Ali as our ruler. Why did you battle him and cause so much bloodshed then?"

2.   Mu'awiyah claims that Allah has blessed him with his right to rule and dominate! Even men like Genghis Khan, Nero and other bloodthirsty tyrants in history did not attribute their oppressions and wrongdoing to Allah, whereas Mu'awiyah, Yazid and Ubayd Allah ibn Ziyad have – as we have already mentioned – stated all of their actions to be Allah's will!

3.   "But you do not accept it." May all Machiavellian ways of deception come to an end! Mu'awiyah admitted on many occasions that people did not want him to be their ruler.

When Mu'awiyah went to Madina – the city where most of the Holy Prophet's friends and disciples were – to impose Yazid as their ruler, he had the elite of the city (including Imam Hussain) come together and delivered a nerve-racking speech which lacked cohesion. Such an action was the mark of those who intend to deceive a society[121] rather than a ruler appointed by the Holy Prophet (PBUH) and in line with divine laws.

Mu'awiyah then praised Yazid and said, "You know Yazid's reputation very well, and you have confirmed and chosen his rule! Allah knows that

---

[120] Ibn Abi l-Hadid, *Sharh Nahjul Balaghah*, Vol. 16

[121] Mu'awiyah said, "Then three men [Abubakr, Umar and Uthman] succeeded the Prophet. There were many cases of demise and downfall which took us a long time to attempt to resolve, whether through observation, or campaigning. About the third man, I only know as much as you do." In contrast to the frankness and honesty Islam has exercised and preached in all individual, social, physical and spiritual aspects, the statements above and Mu'awiyah's deviant behavior can only be interpreted by Machiavelli's works such as *The Discourses* and *The Prince*. As Yaqubi has stated regarding Mu'awiyah's ways of deception in the second volume of his *Tarikh Yaqubi*, "Most of what Mu'awiyah did was based on deception and guile."

by appointing Yazid as the ruler, I mean to have him fill gaps, with open eyes!" After Mu'awiyah continued his fallacies and deceptions for a while, Ibn Abbas was about to retort when Imam Hussain (PBUH) gestured that he should remain silent. Then Imam Hussain (PBUH) himself rose, praised Allah and saluted the Holy Prophet (PBUH), and then added:

> O Mu'awiyah! The light of dawn has shown how black coal is, and the sunlight has made the tiny lights useless. You went too far with what you said, and you violated righteousness... Your words in fact served the Satan... Do you plant to deceive people about your son Yazid?! It seems as if you are describing something hidden, or explaining someone nobody has ever seen before... You think you are saying something only you know about and no one else is aware of at all.
>
> Yazid himself has revealed the truth about him; he has proven what his views and beliefs are. Say about Yazid what he himself admits to and points out his character. His life is all about dogs jumping at each other and attacking one another. He has spent his life just having fun with maids and concubines who sing and dance for him. Stop this; you have had enough of this heavy burden you have been carrying. You have indeed accumulated more than enough evil deeds and wrongdoing to meet your Lord with.
>
> I swear to Allah that all you have been doing so far has been oppression and wrongdoing. Your cup is full. Enough is enough. You are just a blink of an eye away from death ...[122]

Who Appointed Yazid to Rule over People? Was It Allah, Mu'awiyah, or the People?

On two occasions, Mu'awiyah stated that Yazid was appointed to rule by Allah and the people. Such an association indicates quite clearly the sophistry and fallacy Mu'awiyah devised.

1.   Mu'awiyah told Aisha[123],

> Yazid's rule was an act of Allah, and people had no choice but to accept it.

He immediately added,

> The public have accepted his rule and confirmed it. Are you of the opinion that people might break the pledge of allegiance they made regarding Yazid's governance?[124]

---

[122] Ibn Qutaybah al-Dinawari, *Al-Imamah wal Siyasa*, Vol. 1. All well-established Islamic sources have cited the corruption and wrongdoing Yazid committed. Also see Yaqubi's *Tarikh Yaqubi*, Vol. 2.

[123] Aisha bint Abi Bakr, a wife of the Holy Prophet (PBUH). [Translator]

[124] Ibn Qutaybah al-Dinawari, *Al-Imamah wal Siyasa*, Vol. 1.

2. The fallacy and contradiction in Mu'awiyah's words in his conversation with Abdullah ibn Umar (the son of the second Caliph Umar) needs to explanation.[125] If Yazid's rule was decreed by Allah's will, why was there any need for people to make a pledge of allegiance to him? He might even reply that Allah's will was to make Yazid rule because the people wanted him to rule! There are three points to be considered here:

    a. Mu'awiyah's words quite clearly deprive people of any authority, free will or choice concerning Yazid's rule over them. Thus, people's pledge of allegiance with him is not a necessity here.

    b. How could the massive disagreements and oppositions voiced against Yazid in Islamic communities be in line with people's pledge of allegiance to him?

    c. If Allah's will deem something as necessary, why would there be any need for brutal force? There would not unless the Umayyad clan, Mu'awiyah most importantly, claim that they are the only ones who know what Divine Will demands!

3. Mu'awiyah has also admitted that he himself made Yazid the ruler.

Using the strategies of threat and the arousal of greed in people – which were fundamental parts of Mu'awiyah's character – he managed to have his son Yazid succeed him. Then, Mu'awiyah died and went, along with his deeds, to face his maker.

The simple-minded people of Damascus, particularly those who were greedy for the fulfillment of their lusts and desires, created a fake image of Mu'awiyah before and after his death, like a deceiving statue of him before which people bowed like slaves and even made others do the same. However, it did not take long for the real statue-maker of the conscience of history got to work and revealed Mu'awiyah's true face – sword in hand, attacking the statue. While displaying men like Pharaoh, Abu Jahl, Ibn Muljam and Machiavelli on one side of its showcase, the sensitive conscience of history also presents us with Moses, Jesus, Muhammad and Ali (may peace be upon them). Thus, wise analysts and critics of history put Mu'awiyah beside the likes of Machiavelli.

Had Mu'awiyah not appointed his own son Yazid to rule, or had an obstacle come up and prevented Yazid from rising to power, the simple-minded people of that time and now might never have discovered the truth about Mu'awiyah, and would thus have continued bowing before that fake statue made of him. Historical experiences, however, which have always proved to us that the conscience of history is ever awake and alert, once again got to work without the least compromise, flattery or exaggeration, displaying the astounding crimes committed by Mu'awiyah and his son

---

[125] Ibid.

Yazid, thus crying out, "This is who Mu'awiyah was."

The Farm of History Has Always Had Its Springs and Falls

The highly meaningful and fruitful farm of history continually goes through springs and falls. That is a fact; why, however, Allah's will and wisdom has made history that way is a totally different story which this book may be able to explain to some extent. The history we have gone through has experienced ups and downs in the form of mankind drowning in dark ignorance and the emergence of enlightening beliefs and life-saving schools of thought, civilizations and cultures. To find out why history has progressed in such a way, on the other hand, the finest of thoughts and the most divine of feelings are needed.

The same wisdom may also be applicable to man's individual life and his mental state. As Rumi has described it:

> O Brother [who is progressing along Allah's path]! Avoid your natural self for a while;
> even if for a few mere moments, put your ego and your selfishness aside, and join the sea of the "divine self".
> Then you will find yourself in a sea of divine light.
> Do some intuitive soul-searching, and you will see various states arise within you by the moment.
> Indeed, we experience springs and falls inside ourselves.[126]

In other words, if sorrows do not purify us deep inside, joys will never give us any delight. Pain makes human faculties and powers focus more carefully, and alert human beings ponder useful evaluations in their lives; likewise, ideological gaps and distinguished figures can help make alert, conscious people endeavor to guide history toward great virtues.

In short, although there is a great hidden secret behind the ups and downs of history, we can still make use of the parts we see. Of course, we mean the formal ups and downs within human beings rather than destructive sorrows. And when we see that the history of Islam witnesses highly unpleasant events and very saddening autumns, it is because it means to allow Hussain ibn Ali enter the domain of humanity. Likewise, the autumns of the era of the Holy Prophet Abraham and before that served to prepare human beings to meet the great leader Allah had sent them, and the reign of the pharaohs paved the way for the brilliant era of Moses, and the long years of ignorance and decadence in Arabia was followed by the eternal prosperity of Islam. In other words, these destructive autumns led to eternal springs in the foundations of a life based on meritorious virtues.

---

[126] Rumi's *Mathnawi*, Book 1.

Part 15

Who Was Yazid? What Did He Do?

In the case of some figures in history, merely seeing or hearing about a single description of the shameless, extreme oppressions they committed or how seriously they confronted good and righteousness is enough.

Yazid, who was the symbol of wicked evil, hedonist greed and selfishness, is such an example. Let us see what Abdul Rahman ibn Khaldun has written in his work *Al-Muqaddimah* in this regard:

> *What can I say about Hussain? When it was revealed to everyone at that time what corruption and evil Yazid was busy with, the followers of the Holy Prophet's progeny in Kufa asked Hussain, the son of Ali, to go to Kufa and help them rise against Yazid.*

The statement above clearly reveals Yazid's character, for unless one's corruption, villainy and maleficence reach an ultimate, it cannot be claimed that such features existing in a certain person are clearly proven to all, because there can be hundreds of possibilities, interpretations, personal biases and public tendencies preventing the whole population of over ten major Islamic communities – young or old, educated or commoner – to admit the wrongdoing of the most prominent figure among them.

Even regardless of the consensus among the communities in Yazid's time as well as what authorities and scholars thought of him in the following eras and centuries, a careful study of Yazid's administration during the three and a half years he ruled leaves no doubt that if Imam Hussain had made an agreement with him, Islam would definitely have been totally wiped out and the people would have become Umayyad slaves.

Now let us look more closely at Yazid's repertoire:

1. Killing Hussain, the son of Ali, along with 71 other great men in a fashion that no historian, whether Muslim or non-Muslim, have been able to study or write about this event without being terrified, abhorred and experiencing immense mental suffering.
2. The massacre of the residents of Madina. Historians have written that when the bloodthirsty Mongolians ravaged a place, they would arrive, kill everyone, burn the place down and leave, whereas no historian has reported Genghis Khan or Hulagu Khan to have ordered their generals to gather the survivors and have each and every one of them make pledges to be slaves. Yazid did that.

As Yazid instructed his executioner, Mulsim ibn Uqbah, if anyone in

Madina survived, they would have to make a pledge to be Yazid's slave. If they did not do so, they were to be beheaded.[127]

3. Burning down the Kaaba and killing the people of Macca.

This is what Yazid did during his 3.5-year reign.

Having Appointed His Son Yazid to Succeed Him, Mu'awiyah Died and Now Had to Face the Character He Had Created of Himself

Once again, the history of mankind saw a character who had fallen extremely out of line when it comes to the supreme goals and ideals designated for human beings by Islam die. However, since he had appointed his son – who continued his style of governance – to succeed him, his character did not disappear. On the other hand, the obsequious flatterers could not totally wipe away Mu'awiyah's true face from people's memories, or from history for that matter.

Historical records from that era indicate that Mu'awiyah prepared the grounds for his son to rule by means of brutal force or lavish banquets, there is no document in history pointing out that the public – from common people to the elite – willingly accepted Yazid, a man who was second to none when it came to corruption, decadence and lowliness, as their ruler. Indeed, power illegally attained, along with the unawareness of the majority of the public, the empathy instilled into the minds of the common people, the incapability, humility and compromise shown by those who could have potentially been managers of the community, all came together to have Yazid – the son of Mu'awiyah and the man who would later order Hussain, the son of Ali, a symbol of the finest of human and divine virtues, to be killed – rise to power.

Historical records show that even during the reign of Mu'awiyah, who sometimes pretended to observe Islamic rules in his administration, Imam Hussain (PBUH) was continually thinking about how he could find a way to save the community from the power-greedy tyrants of his time. Nonetheless, given the existing circumstances, particularly due to the commitment Imam Hussain (PBUH) had made to Mu'wiyah to avoid extensive bloodshed, he took no action to start a movement or a revolution. Even after the death of his brother, Imam Hassan Mujtaba (PBUH), when the Shiites of Iraq asked Imam Hussain (PBUH) to go there and establish a just Islamic government, Imam Hussain (PBUH) refused and said:

> Mu'awiyah and I made an arrangement. It would not be appropriate
> for me to break this arrangement as long as it is to be respected.
> When Mu'awiyah dies, I will think about it and make a decision.[128]

"I think," Jabir ibn Abdullah told Imam Hussain (PBUH), "that you should make a peace with Yazid, like your brother Hassan Mujtaba who made a peace with Mu'awiyah." Imam Hussain replied, however:

---

[127] Ahmad ibn Abi Yaqub, *Tarikh Yaqubi*, Vol. 2.

[128] Muhaddith Qumi, *Nafas ul-Mahmum.*

*The peace my brother made with Mu'awiyah was ordered by Allah
and the Prophet, and so is my battle against Yazid.*[129]

It Was the Immense Importance of Keeping One's Promise That Made Hussain (PBUH) Remain Silent during Mu'awiyah's Reign

Imam Hussain's silence during the dark era of Mu'awiyah's reign was owing to the commitment made when Imam Hassan Mujtaba (PBUH) was alive in order to avoid confrontation. Hussain (PBUH), a man of the finest of human-divine values and virtues, knew very well how immensely important it was to keep one's promise and that remaining as good as one's word is a virtue worthy of sacrifice. In contrast, Mu'awiyah violated every item of the pact he had made with Imam Hassan (PBUH) regarding the avoidance of war, and in fact acted in conflict with everything he had pledged to do. That was Imam Hussain (PBUH), and this was Mu'awiyah. Mu'awiyah saw everything as serving to further his own power and control over worldly affairs and regarded the promises he made as totally worthless, while Imam Hussain (PBUH) was ready to sacrifice himself in order to fulfill the divine duty he had and what his pure conscience called him to do rather than gain power. His character was the same as Ali ibn Abi Talib's, as was as committed to keeping his pledges and promises as his father was.

As Imam Ali (PBUH) has instructed in his order to Malik Ashtar:

> *O Malik! If you ever make a pact with your enemy, or if you give your adversary a promise of safety, keep good on your promise, and provide the immunity you have pledged to undertake. No matter how varied and diverse the public may be in their desires and tendencies, they agree that arrangements and promises must be respected. This is a well-establishment rule which even non-believers observed, for they had witnessed the undesirable consequences the breaking of a promise may have. Never engage in deceptions to escape the refuge you have promised your enemy and avoid breaking your pledges, for only a foolish tyrant would dare to do such a thing in the presence of Allah. Allah has set the law of pledges, refuge and safety as a blessing for His servants so that life can continue in security and immunity. Therefore, no deception or tricks should be devised. Never make a deal in an obscured, vague way, for that may lead to complications or problems. Once the treaty has been finalized and firmly agreed upon, do not turn to sophistry or guile. And if the promise you make in the presence of Allah leaves you in dire straits, do not let that lead to the dissolution of the arrangement, for if you remain patient and hope for the complications to be resolved, that*

---

[129] Ibid.

*would be much better than your apologizing for the unpleasant
results that you may fear as well the punishment you will face
both in this world and in the afterlife.*[130]

If we do not accept the rule given below regarding the intelligible life of
human beings, the world we live in will be worth no more than sitting and
having fun in a coffee house filled with nihilists: **All governments, both good
and evil, meet their demise after a certain period of time. The only difference
between them is that the main goal of righteous governments is to provide the
finest of virtues as light shining along the path humanity is to progress to achieve
evolution, while evil governments aim to inflate the "animal self" by means of
sacrificing all truths as means to their end. As a result, righteous rulers devote
themselves to providing light for the path toward evolution; not only see their
rule as a means to serve this goal, but in fact they see their own selves as ready for
self-sacrifice to further that goal as well.**

Based on the law expressed above, it is not important how long a
righteous government stays in power or how large a territory it has in
control. For such governments, the presentation and establishments of the
values and virtues of the intelligible life of human beings is of significance.
Evil governments, on the other hand, have only one goal – dominate human
beings and use the physical and spiritual lives of people as a means to
advance the rulers' selfish advancements. Therefore, they devote all of their
resources and potentials into inflating "the natural, animal self" as much as
possible so that they can make their control vaster and indulge further into
their selfish desires.

**After Mu'awiyah's Death, Yazid Wrote a Letter to Walid ibn Utbah, the Governor
of Madina, Ordering Him to Immediately Get Hussain, Ali's Son, to Make a
Pledge of Allegiance to Yazid**

The letter reads:

> *Have Hussain, Abdullah ibn Umar and Abdullah ibn Zubayr
> immediately make a pledge of allegiance to me; do this at once.*[131]

This is how despotic tyrants in charge are; they allow no one any right to
think or exercise any free will. They regard themselves as possessing such
absolute will and authority that not only do they see the free will of other
human beings as dependent upon their permission, but they in fact do not
see others as deserving to live without their allowance! As Rumi has put it:

> *How can man, with his eyes and ears wide open, be so blind?
> Allah has done this, and I am amazed and astonished by it.*[132]

How can they regard any value for the lives of other human beings when
all values are in fact worthless compared to their own desires and wishes!

---

[130] *Nahjulbalaghah*, Letter 53, Imam Ali's Arrangement with Malik Ashtar.

[131] Izzuddin Abul Hassan Muhammad ibn Muhammad Abdul Karim Abdul Wahid
Shaibani, better known as Ibn Al-Athir, *Al-Kamil fil-Tarikh*, Vol. 4.

[132] Rumi's *Mathnawi*, Book 3.

Part 16

The Goals and Incentives Which Made the Intense
Resistance and the Campaign of Imam Hussain (PBUH)
Take a Formal, Disclosed Approach

Some who lack information and have merely made a superficial study of the history of Islam assume that Imam Hussain's resistance and campaign began when Mu'awiyah died and Yazid succeeded him. Such an assumption is definitely in contrast with the truth. The campaign and movement Imam Hussain (PBUH) started has roots much deeper than being originated with the rise of Yazid to power.

After the Holy Prophet passed away, Imam Hussain (PBUH), the son of Ali (PBUH) and the master of all martyrs of righteousness and truth, was involved in all of the ups and down the Islamic society experienced, and witnessed with total awareness and sensitivity how crucial the occurring events were. Hussain did not suddenly open his eyes to find Yazid's letter being read out to him asking him to submit unconditionally to the despotic tyranny set up by Yazid's father Mu'awiyah. This son of the founders of Islam did not come across Yazid and the likes of Yazid all of a sudden. Imam Hussain (PBUH) had been silently and painfully watching this go on for long years. Why? Let us take into consideration a few examples of the fierce, autumn winds which were ravaging the enlightening, beautiful garden of Islam and deeply upset him:

- Imam Hussain (PBUH) witnessed the terrible hardships brought about for his father Ali ibn Abi Talib (PBUH). The only reasons for such inconveniences were lust for authority and power, the need to fulfill one's whims and desires and jealousy.
- He heard what his dear father said due to the suffering and emotional experiences he went through.
- Imam Hussain (PBUH) could never forget what his father had said – "I tolerated it, although I felt dust in my eyes and sorrow in my throat."[133]
- He had seen how others' Machiavellian policies had ravaged and destroyed some of his father's faithful friends, human beings of the highest of virtues. A few of these great men were:
1. With tearful eyes and a heavy heart, Imam Hussain (PBUH) had seen off Abu-Dhar al-Ghifari, a man who had been exiled for advocating

---

[133] *Nahjulbalaghah*, Sermon 3.

reforms and adjustments in people's lives and defending the school of thought of "equal right", one of the most human basics of Islam.

2.   Then one day, Ali (PBUH) lost Ammar ibn Yasir as well. Historians have all reported that the Holy Prophet (PBUH) had said:

O Ammar! You will be killed by a group of oppressive wrongdoers.

Ammar was killed during the Siffin battles. When Imam Ali (PBUH) had Mu'awiyah and his men reminded about the Holy Prophet's prediction regarding Ammar's fate, the follower of Machiavellian styles came up with an answer which is so nihilistic and futile that it has astounded history! Mu'awiyah said, "It was Ali who killed Ammar; after all, Ali brought him to this battlefield!"

Let us quote from Rumi once again:

How can man, with his eyes and ears wide open, be so blind?
Allah has done this, and I am amazed and astonished by it.[134]

Imam Ali then said:

Then tell them that it was the Prophet who killed Hamzah, the son of Abdul Muttalib, for the Prophet had brought him to the battlefield as well.

3.   Then the day came when Imam Hussain (PBUH) heard that Malik Ashtar had been poisoned to death! Who was Malik Ashtar? While he was one of the greatest and the bravest warriors history has ever seen, Malik was also an extremely pious, spiritual man. He was one of the very few men who had truly "known" Ali. When Malik died in the unfair, wrongful way he did, Ali – a pillar of patience and endurance – began weeping. Having heard that this great man had been poisoned on Mu'awiyah's orders on his way to Egypt, Imam Ali cried:

O Malik! What a man he was! And now there is no Malik. May he rest in peace; indeed, he was to me what I was to the Holy Prophet.

Malik was the man who deserved to receive Imam Ali's famous instructions to govern the ancient land of Egypt. Imam Ali's plan was so rich and comprehensive that it could be used to manage and cause improvement in any country.

4.   He knew about Hujr and his men – some of the finest men of the Islamic society – being killed even though Mu'awiyah had promised them immunity. Imam Hussain (PBUH) found it quite painful not only to bear the sorrow of the loss of such great men, but also the fact that those who had brought about such irreparable damage regarded what they had done as an ingenious act of the art of governance!

---

[134] Rumi's *Mathnawi*, Book 3.

5. Uwais al-Qarani, a man whose great spirit had made the Holy Prophet (PBUH) think highly of him. The Holy Prophet (PBUH) even went on to describe him as:

I can smell a divine breath from Yemen.

Abu Sa'id Abul Khayr has also depicted their relationship in his poetry:

> *To be with me, you need to have passion and an attentive heart; otherwise, even if you are beside me, you will in fact be quite remote. I also have great passion for you, so great that we have become one; I see no difference between us.*

Uwais became a victim of the greed for authority and desire for power of Mu'awiyah and his followers. Thus, dozens – and maybe even hundreds – of great seekers of truth who were followers of Ali (PBUH) were killed. Hussain, Ali's son, witnessed all of these and knew how they suffered.

6. Imam Hussain (PBUH) had witnessed all of the oppression, wrongdoing and infringement the world-worshipping tyrants made his brother Imam Hassan Mujtaba (PBUH) suffer from. Indeed, he endured a great deal of pain and hardships in many ways.

7. He saw Islamic laws and values being violated using skills and ways of deception which the common public could not fathom. Therefore, Imam Hussain (PBUH) was unable to make the majority of the people realize what wrongdoing was taking place and thus start a campaign against it. This was why Imam Hassan Mujtaba (PBUH) preferred to make a pact to avoid war rather than engage in battle.

8. Human dignity and respect was being violated, and people's honor was being sacrificed to advance the selfish desires of a few. People were regarded as mindless slaves, and the views and wishes of the public were considered as worthless. The motto was, "People are a bunch of helpless animals, and I can do as I please about them!" Such a mindset, leaves nothing left of humanity.

In the Holy Quran, Allah, on the other hand, has seen consultation as one of the most fundamental pillars of Islam:

And consult them in affairs.[135]

* * *

... those who conduct their affairs by mutual consultation.[136]

The Truth Is a Massive Tree Whose Branches Lie within Pure People

It is an eternal order of man's reason and conscience that the fruits on these branches, which exist in the hearts and wisdoms of pure human beings,

---

[135] The Family of Imran (3:159).
[136] Consultation (42:38).

should be used. Consultation is the same point reworded – we must use the fruits of people's reason, wisdom and hearts.

Part 17

The Role of the Leader's Piety in His Management of the Society and His Justification of His Actions

Let us see how Islam's eternal logic regarding the qualities of a leader have been described in the words of Imam Ali (PBUH), and then discuss the reason for Imam Hussain's uprising. Imam Ali (PBUH) has stated that:

> *Do not give me pleasant praise for the duty I fulfill. Releasing one's character from the claws of desires and lusts and guiding it toward Allah and you [who are manifests of Allah's will] calls for no appreciation. I am doing nothing but providing you with the individual and social rights you have in life due to the human-divine assignment I have been given, and I have not even completed that assignment yet. I am carrying out the mandatory, essential duties I have. Your discourse with me should be like your discourse with tyrants. Before me, avoid restraining yourselves or giving in like you used to when facing aggressive men of power. Do not talk to me in a pretentious manner. Do not think that I will balk at something righteous said to me; I shall never regard myself as superior to what is righteous, for he who finds it too difficult to listen to what is righteous will never be able to act in justice and righteousness. Before me, do not avoid speaking out what is right or providing me with consultation so as to help make justice a reality. Unless Allah – Who owns me in a much more superior way than how I own myself – helps me, I am not a character beyond error. There is no doubt that you and I are servants and belongings of the One Allah. He is the Absolute Owner of our souls; His ownership is much superior to our ownership of our own selves. It is Allah Who has brought us from the very lowly stages of life up to the highest levels, and turned our blindness and ignorance into enlightening.*[137]

When Imam Hussain (PBUH) – as the realization and materialization of the Islamic logic and reason depicted in the above statements – witnesses the deterioration of this logic and sees it being replaced by arrogance, selfishness, despotism, racism, decadent and ignorant prejudices, when he sees the lives

---

[137] *Nahjulbalaghah*, Sermon 216.

of Islamic societies falling in the hands of Yazid – whose reputation after three years of ruling is quite clear – should he not take action in order to save Islam?! Although Mu'awiyah's death was of very high importance for his men, what Walid saw as an extremely significant task was to make Imam Hussain (PBUH), Abdullah ibn Umar and Abdullah ibn Zubayr make a pledge of allegiance to – and in fact surrender to – Yazid. Thus, Walid ibn Utbah sent for Marwan ibn Al-Hakam. When Marwan arrived, Walid read out to Marwan the letter announcing Mu'awiyah's death and Yazid's command that the three men mentioned above must be obliged to make a pledge of allegiance. Then he asked Marwan what he thought about Yazid's order. "I think," Marwan said, "that you should summon all three of them right now and have them make their pledge of allegiance to Yazid. If they refuse to do so, you must behead them even before they learn about Mu'awiyah's death! If they find out that Mu'awiyah is dead, they will each go somewhere and make attempts to take control."

It is a proven principle that excessive affection and kindness can make man's life fall astray from the path of "intelligible life"; the same goes for excessive adversity, which is also indicative of mental disorder.

Marwan's animosity toward the Holy Prophet's clan rooted way back to pre-Islamic times. Historical sources and *hadith* provide accounts and records for this intense enmity.

In response to Walid's question about what they were to do regarding Yazid's orders, Marwan displays his anti-human nature and, quite bluntly, states that Imam Hussain (PBUH) must be murdered! His answer not only indicates his adversity toward Islam, but it also shows how ignorant he is toward all human values. Kill Hussain ibn Ali (PBUH)! Who is Hussain ibn Ali? He is the son of Fatimah (PBUH), the Holy Prophet's daughter. He was, as seen by all conscientious authorities, the best man to establish a righteous government which could uphold justice; he had the greatest capability and capital when it came to nurturing and developing human beings. Killing him as a political move would not mean just the destruction of a human being, but in fact the most dangerous manipulation possible in the history of mankind and demolishing the rights of human souls. Sometimes the revival of an individual who has great virtues leads to the revival of all human beings, even though the man who ordered the revival may not have realized the importance of what he has done. Likewise, sometimes ordering that someone be killed may in fact be the demise of the whole of mankind, no matter whether the person issuing the decree is aware of such an equation or not. Of course, if the issuer of the command does not know of this and is not to blame in this unawareness, however, the burden of responsibility will not be as serious.

Can it be imagined that Marwan, who ordered that Imam Hussain (PBUH) be killed, did not know such a divine, distinguished figure? What made Marwan, who lived in the Islamic community and could have been informed of the characters of Imam Hussain and Yazid, fail to know them? If such issues remain historically vague and unclear parts of history,

the credibility of this important phenomenon known as history will be
diminished.

Walid ibn Utbah Sent Someone to Summon Hussain (PBUH), Abdullah ibn Umar and Abdullah ibn Zubayr and Get Them to Make a Pledge of Allegiance to Yazid

Walid's dispatch, a young man called Abdullah ibn Amr ibn Uthman,
found Imam Hussain (PBUH) and Zubayr's son sitting in the mosque. It
was not the time people were commonly summoned to see Walid. Walid's
dispatch delivered his message, however, and said, "The Commander has
summoned you." "You can go back," the two men replied, "we shall go to
see Walid later." Then, Ibn Zubayr asked Imam Hussain (PBUH), "What do
you think? This is not the usual time Walid sees people. Why has he called
for us?" "I believe that wrongdoer, Mu'awiyah, has died," Imam Hussain
replied, "and Walid wants to have us make a pledge of allegiance before
the news gets out." "That is exactly what I think," Abdullah ibn Zubayr
agreed.[138] Then he asked Imam Hussain (PBUH), "What are you going to
do?" "I shall gather a few young men from my family," the Imam answered,
"and position them around Walid's place. Then, I will go in." "I fear that
Walid may be conspiring against you," Abdullah said. "I will not go there
without having prepared to defend myself first," Imam Hussain (PBUH)
replied.[139]

---

[138] Ibn Al-Athir, *Al-Kamil fil-Tarikh*, Vol. 4.
[139] Ibid.

Part 18

The Law of Aggressively Defending One's Life

The measures taken by Imam Hussain (PBUH) to prepare to defend himself against Walid bin Utbah imply the importance of preparation in defense of one's life; indeed, Imam Ali's son had taken the defense of life and avoiding entering a fatal battle as a serious law. Some of those who lack information have assumed that Imam Hussain (PBUH) should not have resisted the powerful and fully equipped Yazid and that Imam Hussain's resistance and campaign against the tyrant of his era was a mistake; such an assumption is clearly wrong. Even Ibn Khaldun has made such a mistake as well:

> *Hussain felt that it was absolutely necessary to fight the corrupt,*
> *wrongdoing Yazid; indeed, particularly if one had the capability*
> *to start such a campaign, and Hussain saw himself as capable. He*
> *assumed himself able enough and deserving enough [to rule the*
> *Islamic society], and he was right, even more than he had assumed.*
> *As for his military capability, however, he was not as powerful as he*
> *had assumed.*[140]

Ibn Khaldun's mistake in the theory he has presented can be clearly seen in Imam Hussain's remark on visiting Walid. Indeed, Imam Hussain (PBUH) has truly expressed the law of aggressive defense of one's life here. Let us take the Imam's words into careful consideration once again:

> *I shall not face Walid unless I am capable of defending myself.*

It is a pity that Ibn Khaldun, with all of his knowledge and powerful intellect, has failed to accurately understand the meaning of power as seen by common sense, man's perfection-seeking essence and Islamic sources!

As confirmed by common sense, man's perfection-seeking essence and Islamic sources, committing oneself to martyrdom along the path of intelligible life is one of the finest examples of power, and Imam Hussain (PBUH) had power at its highest level possible.

With such power, Imam Hussain (PBUH) saw himself as seriously responsibility in regard to the history of humanity, helpless lives and, most important of all, in the presence of Allah.

There is immense difference between Imam Hussain's going to see Walid

---

[140] Ibn Khaldun, *Muqaddimah.*

ibn Utbah – for which Imam Hussain (PBUH) had completely prepared himself so as to safeguard values and virtues – and his serious uprising against Yazid, Mu'awiyah's son and the tyrant of his time. In the first event (going to see Walid) merely involved natural preparations, for if he were to secretly have been killed within a house – an incident which may have led to highly varied interpretations and justifications – the results would not have even the slightest impact in releasing the people of the communities of that time from the slave-like life Yazid had imposed upon them. On the other hand, a formal movement and campaign along with raising awareness among people about the serious problems their physical and spiritual life was suffering from because of the despotic Yazid, as well as the various events which began from Madina and continued up to Imam Hussain's return to Madina, was the greatest means and power Allah had granted Imam Hussain (PBUH). It is obvious, however, that those who consider power and incapability from a highly superficial point of view will fail to understand such a notion of power. Due to this principle of aggressive defense of life:

> Hussain gathered a group of his family members and his friends around him and had them armed. 'Walid has summoned me,' he told them, 'and he may demand something which I cannot do. He is not reliable. When I go inside to see him, stay near the door. If I raise my voice, come in and defend me.'[141]

This is indeed the main logic and philosophy underlying life which Allah has blessed human beings with. If man is in possession of the whole material world but he does not use it in order to defend even the last second of his life, he has failed to understand life as well as the material world.

> Imam Hussain went to see Walid. Marwan was with Walid as well. Walid informed Imam Hussain that Mu'awiyah had died. Imam Hussain recited the verse of the Quran regarding how humans returned to their Creator after death ("Verily, to Allah we belong, and to Allah we will return"[142]). Then Walid read out Yazid's letter, which ordered him to get Imam Hussain (PBUH) to make a pledge of allegiance to Yazid. 'I do not believe that you will be content with my secretly making a pledge of allegiance with Yazid,' Imam Hussain (PBUH) said. Walid confirmed the Imam's words. 'Then sleep on it and tell me your decision in the morning,' Imam Hussain (PBUH) said. 'Go back in the name of Allah,' Walid replied, 'and the next time you come to me, have the people accompany you.' Then Marwan told Walid, 'I swear to Allah that if Hussain does not make that pledge of allegiance to you at this very hour and leaves now, you will never be able to prevail over such a character again, unless a great deal of

---

[141] Haj Shaikh Abbas Qumi, *Nafas ul-Mahmum*.
[142] The Cow (2:156).

blood is shed and many souls die. Either keep Hussain detained here so that you can keep him under your control, or behead him![143]

When Imam Hussain (PBUH) tells Walid to wait until morning and then announce his decision, highly significant concepts are indicated – the road to ponder one's responsibility, think about how history may judge one's actions, the prevalence of one's conscience, standing before Allah at the beginning of eternity, etc. In other words, Imam Hussain is in fact saying, "O Walid! The next few hours will be the most crucial and decisive moments of your life. You can make a decision which will guide the fate of Muslim societies toward prosperity and happiness; on the other hand, you might choose a path which will put you among the bloodthirsty tyrants of history who have brought about oppression and atrocity. Go and spend the rest of today and tonight thinking on your final decision. In your contemplations, you will have to face human principles, the judgment your predecessors and future generations will make about you, the consequences your actions will result in, and most important of all, Allah. You and I are both at the turning points of our lives and our destinies here today. O Walid! Go and think. These hours will not come again. Your eternal happiness or doom will be the outcome of how you think within the next few hours. I am leaving now, and there is no doubt that we will both see how we will be remembered in the face of the great showcase of history, and we will also eventually come across once again when it comes to Allah's judgment of us."

Furthermore, Walid told Imam Hussain to "Go back in the name of Allah." If only Walid had included himself among those who should act in the name of Allah as well; had he acted on this divine name, had he said, "Walid, tonight you must face your own self in the name of Allah," he may have brought about the most beautiful and the most constructive consequences possible regarding his own destiny.

During his encounter with Imam Hussain's divine character, Walid experienced an enlightening flash of conscience; thus, he allowed Imam Hussain (PBUH) to leave. Walid did not force the Imam to do anything, and did not humiliate or insult him in any way, either. When Imam Hussain (PBUH) had left, Marwan once again displayed his evil, atrocious nature. "You ignored my suggestion," Marwan said. "You failed to get him to make a pledge of allegiance, and when he refused to give in, you did not kill him. Now you will never be able to win him over…"

Walid replied:

> *I swear to Allah that even if I were given all of the wealth and possessions in the world in return for killing Hussain just because he refused to make a pledge of allegiance with Yazid, I would never commit such a crime. I swear to Allah that anyone who has Hussain's blood on his hands will have a very little chance to gain Allah's*

---

[143] Haj Shaikh Abbas Qumi, *Nafas ul-Mahmum.*

approval on Judgment Day.[144]

"The statements above indicate that the flash of conscience Walid had experienced was to some extent deeply rooted, for Walid must have had great reverence for the greatness of Imam Hussain (PBUH) to have come up with such a highly impressive response to Marwan. "[145]

"That is true," Marwan said. Although this wicked man seemed to agree, his was not being quite sincere; Marwan was not happy about what Walid had said.[146]

In regard to Marwan's pretending to agree that Walid had been right, two possibilities can be pointed out. First, he may have been acting on one of Yazid's famous poems:

> *Hashim's clan are merely playing along in order to gain power pretentiously;*
> *in fact, there has been no revelation of any kind!*

In other words, Marwan may have been mocking Walid. "Yes, keep believing that," Marwan may have meant, "Hussain is out of your control now, and in order to prevail over him, a great deal of blood will have to be shed."

A second possibility is that Marwan was, regardless of Yazid's beliefs, merely putting Walid up to ridicule, as if to say, "Very well… we will see!"

Muhaddith Qumi has thus quoted an account of this event from Ibn Shahr Ashoub:

> *When Imam Hussain came to see Walid ibn Utbah, Walid read Yazid's letter out for him. Imam Hussain said, 'I refuse to pledge my allegiance to Yazid.'*
> *'Join sides with the Commander of the Faithful!" Marwan said.*
> *'That is a lie,' Imam Hussain replied. 'Who appointed Yazid as the commander of the faithful?'*
> *Marwan drew his sword and told Walid, 'Have your executioner behead Hussain before he can leave this house. Hold me liable for his blood.'*
> *Shouts were heard from inside Walid's house, and at that moment, 19 men from Hussain's family, armed with daggers, entered. Hussain left the house accompanied by them. When Yazid learned about what had happened, Walid was fired and Marwan succeeded him as the*

---

[144] Ibid. Also see Al-Alayli, Abdullah, *Sumaw Al-Ma'na Fi Sumuw Ath-That Aw Ashi'ah Min Hayat Al-Hussain* ("The Loftiness of the Meaning in the Loftiness of the Essence, or Rays from the Life of Hussain").

[145] Haj Shaikh Abbas Qumi, *Nafas ul-Mahmum.*

[146] Ibid.

governor of Madina.[147]

In any case, Walib ibn Utbah's compassionate conduct toward Imam Hussain (PBUH) made him lose the shameful mission that had been given to him.

An interesting point about this amazing story is the wickedness displayed by Marwan and the flattery and praise he offers regarding Yazid, giving him the title of "the commander of the faithful" in the presence of Imam Hussain (PBUH)! Yazid, the Commander of the Faithful? Which faithful are those who are to be led by Yazid? Yazid was so unworthy of becoming the ruler that even swords and fatal threats did not help Mu'awiyah get people to make a pledge of allegiance to his precious son.

Of course, when politics means that all human and divine principles and virtues are justified or sacrificed along the path of "I am the end, while others are the means", Yazid becomes the commander of the faithful as well!

It is such shameful acts of sycophancy which in fact sharpens the swords of bloodthirsty executioners and tyrants of history, thus making it impossible for human beings of pure hearts and clear consciences to feel shame when they go through pages of history, for all they find is accounts of the bloody suffering and pain mankind has gone through.

From the day after he refused to make a pledge of allegiance to Yazid at Walid ibn Utbah's house, Imam Hussain (PBUH) would hear about what was going on when he came out of his residence. Seeing Imam Hussain, Marwan said, "O Aba Abdillah! I only want the best for you. Take my advice and you will get to where you should get."

"What advice is that?" Imam Hussain asked. "Tell me, and I shall listen."

"I recommend that you take Yazid's side," Marwan said. "That will provide you with prosperity both in this world and in the afterworld!"

Imam Hussain (PBUH) replied:

> *We are from Allah, and we all return to Allah. We should bid Islam a last farewell, for a shepherd like Yazid has taken the nation like a plague. I heard my grandfather say that it is religiously and legally forbidden for Abu Sufyan's offspring to rise to caliphate.*[148]

It would be wrong to assume that Marwan did not know what kind of

---

[147] Ibid, reported from Ibn Shahr Ashoub, *Al-Manaqib.*

Note: Since the main goal of this book is to analytically interpret the martyrdom of Imam Hussain, the martyr of the pioneer culture of humanity, we will not go into detail regarding what happened to Abdullah ibn Zubayr, Abdullah ibn Umar and other people capable of making remarks about Yazid's rule, for Imam Hussain (PBUH) had a divine goal, endeavor and determination for sacrifice so as to revive Islam far greater than anyone else could manage. Our intention in this book is, as you have seen, to portray the most brilliant figure mankind has ever encountered when it comes to sacrificing himself to safeguard the finest of human virtues as well as bearing the most intolerable hardships humanity can imagine.

[148] Muhaddith Qumi, *Nafas ul-Mahmum.*

character Yazid was and recommended that Imam Hussain (PBUH) should seek prosperity and happiness both in this world and in the afterworld through making a pledge of allegiance with him, for it had become quite clear ever since the reign of Mu'awiyah what kind of man Yazid was. At a gathering of the Muslim elite, Mu'awiyah had threatened everyone with his sword in order to establish Yazid as his successor, and had then praised Yazid. "What do you mean by that, O Mu'awiyah?" Imam Hussain (PBUH) had said. "It's as if you are speaking of a man whom no one knows about. You had better describe your son based on what is clear about him..." Moreover, Marwan was a close relative of Yazid's, so it would be impossible for him not to have known what type of man Yazid was!

Nevertheless, Marwan insisted that Imam Hussain's prosperity in his life in this world as well as his afterlife lay in his pledge of allegiance to Yazid!

What kind of worldly life would that be indeed? A life consisted of some years breathing, eating, sleeping, outpours of rage, and indulging into one's lusts and desires, a life empty of dignity or honor, a life in which man only submits to the animal desires of other selfish, despotic tyrants is in fact not life – it is death accompanied by the torture of an aimless life filled with grief, boredom and decadence engulfed in a futile fast headed for an even more futile future. For a man of wisdom, divine conscience and awareness, that is not life, and it has no prosperity or good, either.

If one's prosperity and good lies in surrendering to a man who denies the afterlife, a man who could not care less about the afterworld, then we should define what the afterworld is and what afterlife really mean!

> O Brother [who is progressing along Allah's path]! Avoid your natural self for a while;
> even if for a few mere moments, put your ego and your selfishness aside, and join the sea of the "divine self".
> Then you will find yourself in a sea of divine light.
> Do some intuitive soul-searching, and you will see various states arise within you by the moment.
> Indeed, we experience springs and falls inside ourselves.[149]

The diversity inside human nature is a fact all thinkers, scholars of the humanities, poets and mystics have realized and been fascinated by. Rumi has pointed out such spiritual changes on many occasions, attributing them – provided that they not be wicked or corrupt – to Allah, thus regarding the human soul as similar to nature. The external world undergoes springs and autumns, is sometimes full of life and blooming and sometimes depressed and down, which is exactly what the human spirit experiences as well. But what is the incentive behind such developments? Moreover, are such changes the same in various stages of man's life? Does every human being

---

[149] Rumi's *Mathnawi*, Book 1.

experience all kinds of such changes? Do these changes serve to enhance man's character? Are the joys, sorrows, thoughts and feelings we feel in fact all the same, or are they different? All of these are highly significant psychological issues. However, unfortunately, they have not yet been dealt with, while anthropology cannot proceed without the answers to the questions above! A large group are busy, on the other hand, trying to make people engage in activities that provide them with mere enjoyment, thus making their futile and pointless life in fact seem valuable and precious!

It should be carefully noted that when Imam Hussain (PBUH) stated that he had heard his grandfather, the Holy Prophet (PBUH), say that it is religiously illegal for Abu Sufyan's offspring to ever rule, Marwan did not reply, "No, the Holy Prophet never said anything like that. Has anyone else heard him say that?" Marwan just angrily left.

The evening of that day came, and Walid sent men to summon Imam Hussain (PBUH) and have him make his pledge of allegiance to Yazid. "Let us wait until morning," Imam Hussain told them. "You shall see, and we shall see as well." The men did not insist any further and took no action that night.

That very night – which was the night before a Sunday and there were only two days left until the end of the month of Rajab – Imam Hussain left Madina for Macca along with his children, his brothers, his nieces and nephews and other major relatives except Muhammad ibn Hanafiyyah. When learning about his brother's decision to leave Madina, although he had no idea where his brother's destination was, Muhammad ibn Hanafiyyah said, "You are the best human being here, and you are the most precious person of all to me. I have never given anyone such sincere advice for their own good, but you deserve it. Avoid making a pledge of allegiance to Yazid. Stay away from cities as much as possible. Then, send your men to people and invite them to join you and defend righteousness and justice. If people take your side, you will be grateful to Allah, and if they take sides with someone else, Allah will not allow your religion or wisdom to diminish for that, and your virtues and values will still be intact. What I fear that you may arrive in a city and the people may fall into a disagreement over you, some taking your side and some opposing you. Then, a massacre will occur, and the best human being in the nation regarding the character of his parents will become the most worthless, humiliated one."

> *"Where should I go then, my brother?" Imam Hussain (PBUH) asked Muhammad ibn Hanafiyyah. "Go to Macca first," Muhammad replied. "If you find it a safe haven, that will be your best bet. If not, head toward Yemen. If Yemen gives you the safety you need, that will be your destination. Otherwise, head for deserts and oases within the mountains. Move from one city to another, waiting to see what the people do. With such moves and waits, you shall find out what the best strategy is."*

"You have good intentions, my brother," Imam Hussain (PBUH)
said. "I appreciate your kind advice. I hope you are right."[150]

The late scholar, Majlisi, has added another statement of Imam Hussain's to his account of the conversation above. He has reported that Imam Hussain (PBUH) also said, "I swear to Allah, dear brother, that even if I find nowhere safe to settle, I shall not make a pledge of allegiance to Yazid."[151]

We shall now discuss a few highly important points regarding Imam Hussain's conversation with his brother.

1. Imam Hussain (PBUH) compelled neither Muhammad ibn Hanafiyyah nor anyone else to join him on the move he was about to make.

Nowadays, it might be impossible to imagine that one's children, brothers, nieces, nephews, and one's most prominent family members be like links connected to the chain of one's very being, forming one's character. This is a natural phenomenon brought about by the machine-like lifestyle of today, which is quite averse to life. There is no cure available to take mankind back to the original communication and interaction they intelligibly used to have, either – unless those in charge of the technological world of today could wake up from the heavy sleep of lust for wealth and greed for dominance they have submersed themselves in and take into consideration once again man, the human spirit, the human character and human virtues, and give human beings their identity back. There is no wonder why authorities on sociology have called our era the era of human beings' alienation toward one another, an era which has resulted in the disease of self-alienation. When it comes to the natural, reasonable relationship a group of human beings have with one another, the greater the individual characters' personalities are, the more intimate the relationships will be; could one find a man greater than Imam Hussain (PBUH), a man whose brothers, nephews, nieces and other relatives found life an intolerable disgrace after his wrongful martyrdom. The history of that era clearly indicates that Imam Hussain's close relatives were not the only ones to feel life an eternal, painful disgrace after his martyrdom; a group of prominent figures of that time, known as the *tawwabin* ("the repentant ones"), including men like Sulaiman ibn Surad Khaza'i (a disciple of the Holy Prophet), Musayyib ibn Najiyyah Fazari (a friend of Imam Ali's), Abdullah ibn Sa'id Asadi, Abdullah ibn Wal Tamimi and Rafa'at ibn Shaddad Bajali, eager to wash away the pain of having not rushed to help Imam Hussain (PBUH), began a campaign and fought as hard as they could, willing to even sacrifice their lives.

As Sulaiman ibn Surad told a group of *tawwabin*:

You should be like the children of Israel, whose prophet said to them,

---

[150] Muhaddith Qumi, *Nafas ul-Mahmum*. Also see Ibn Al-Athir, *Al-Kamil fil-Tarikh*, Vol. 4.
[151] Majlisi, Allamah Muhammad Baqir, *Bihar ul-Anwar*, the volume regarding Imam Hussain.

> *O my people, indeed you have wronged yourselves by your taking of the calf [for worship].*[152]
> **So, repent to your Creator and kill yourselves.**[153]

Moreover, as Khalid ibn Nafil put it:

> *I swear to Allah that if I were sure that suicide would save me from this guilt I feel, I would kill myself.*[154]

Given such intense zeal and enthusiasm when it comes to defending and supporting Imam Hussain (PBUH), they would definitely have rushed to his aid had they known for sure that the Nainawa event was going to take place.

Thus, the departure of Imam Hussain's children, brothers, nephews, nieces and prominent relatives and their accompanying him was absolutely at their own choice and out of free will. Moreover, Muhammad ibn Hanfiyyah may have prepared to accompany his brother as well, but Imam Hussain (PBUH) may have ordered him to stay in Madina. The letter below, which has been written by Imam Hussain (PBUH) and quoted and reported by Imam Sadiq (PBUH), also depicts the fact that Imam Hussain (PBUH) did not force anyone to go with him.

Hamzah bin Hamran has reported that he was once in Imam Sadiq's presence, and Imam Sadiq (PBUH) was speaking about Imam Hussain's departure for Macca and the fact that Muhammad ibn Hanafiyyah was not with him. "When Imam Hussain decided to leave," Imam Sadiq (PBUH) said, "he asked for a piece of paper, and this is what he wrote:

> **In the Name of Allah, the Compassionate, the Merciful.**
> **This is a letter from Hussain, the son of Abi Talib, to the Bani Hashim clan. Whoever of you joins me will be martyred, and whoever defies me will not succeed. May Allah bless you all.**

Indeed, may Allah bless Imam Hussain, the martyr of the path of the truth. Can there be any triumph greater than what he achieved? Although considering how his bloody movement seemed to be, given the ordinary concepts for failure and triumph, it appears to have ended in a superficial failure, Imam Hussain (PBUH) in fact revived Islam, human honor, human dignity and man's natural essence. Had the selfish men in power and the world-greedy enemies of human nature and conscience not prevented the secrets of Imam Hussain's movement from being discovered, revealed and explored, the history of mankind could be on an evolutionary path today.

It is a shame how these owl-like residents of slums have no idea how high eagles can fly; when one can soar like an eagle, there is no point in paying attention to the ruins these decadent beings are so passionate about.

---

[152] Muhaddith Qumi, *Nafas ul-Mahmum*.

[153] The Holy Quran, The Cow (2:54).

[154] Muhaddith Qumi, *Nafas ul-Mahmum*.

Alas, it is impossible to prove to bat-like residents of the dark how the sun works.

It is a pity that these unwise wrongdoers, by concealing the life-saving sacrifices made by Imam Hussain (PBUH), are in fact not only betraying themselves but also committing crimes toward others as well.

With their decadent wickedness and their ignorance, they are trying to cover up the brilliant sun using the dust raised by their lusts and desires! They think they can eliminate, through their ill-minded hallucinations, the truth and righteousness from the hearts of pure human beings – which are only enlightened by the light of Allah – and make them forget about Hussain (PBUH) totally. Indeed, there can be no punishment higher than that which is the consequence of such ignorance and decadence; the mental disease which makes human beings fight their very own selves deserved the highest punishment of all!

2. The words of Muhammad ibn Hanafiyyah, which can be seen as the point of view of all alert, pure Muslims involved in that era, indicate the necessity of Imam Hussain's avoiding taking sides with Yazid and making this intention clear by moving from one city to another, from one desert to another, or from one hiding place within the mountains to another.

Thus, given Yazid's character, the fact that he did not deserve to rule the Islamic society, and his taking advantage of the public's lack of knowledge and awareness as an effort to establish his own power on one side, and considering Imam Hussain's unique personality, his absolute popularity among the people and the fact that the faithful saw him as the best choice to rule, it was quite obvious for Muhammad ibn Hanafiyyah to reiterate that Imam Hussain (PBUH) should avoid making a pledge of allegiance to Yazid.

3. There is a reason why Muhammad ibn Hanafiyyah has suggested that, if finding Macca or Yemen too unsafe to settle in, Imam Hussain (PBUH) should move from one city to another quickly rather than staying in a certain city, or even take to deserts. Such a move would arouse the public's curiosity, and prove the fact that Imam Hussain (PBUH) did not intend to make a pledge of allegiance to Yazid.

Thus, Yazid's deceptions are revealed to the public, and the people in the society become aware of what transcribes behind the curtains. As we shall narrate further on, Imam Hussain (PBUH) told his brother Muhammad ibn Hanafiyyah, "I am ready to leave with my brothers, my nephews, and my Shiite followers. You stay here in Madina, and keep a close eye on what goes on. Keep me posted on everything..." We therefore see that Muhammad ibn hanafiyyah had probably suggested that he also accompany his brother, but Imam Hussain (PBUH) asked him to stay.

As Majlisi has reported:

> *After Imam Hussain (PBUH) had talked with Walid ibn Utbah and before his departure from Madina, Imam Hussain (PBUH) left his*

*house one night and visited the grave of the Holy Prophet (PBUH).
'May Allah's Peace and Blessing be upon you, O Prophet of Allah!'
he said. 'I am Hussain, the son of Fatima, your offspring, the son of
your daughter. I am your grandson. O Prophet of Allah! See how
they humiliated me and let me down. They treated me unrightfully,
and this is what I am complaining to you about, until the day I see
you.' Then Imam Hussain began praying. Walid, on the other hand,
sent someone to Imam Hussain's house to find out whether he had
left Madina or not. He was told that Imam Hussain (PBUH) was
not in Madina. Walid thanked Allah that he did not have Imam
Hussain's blood on his hands. The following night, Imam Hussain
(PBUH) visited the Holy Prophet's grave once again, and did plenty
of praying. Then he raised his hands and said:*

*'O Allah! This is the grave where Your Prophet lies, and I am the son
of the daughter of Your Prophet. You know very well what has been
going on for me. O Allah! I love goodness and I hate evil. For the sake
of this grave and the man buried inside it, Allah, I ask you to allow to
happen to me whatever You think is best.'*

*When it was almost dawn, Imam Hussain (PBUH) had a dream. He
saw the Holy Prophet (PBUH) surrounded by a group of angels. The
Holy Prophet pressed Imam Hussain to his chest, kissed his forehead
and said: 'My dear Hussain! I can see you somewhere near here, and
you are covered with your own blood. In an area known as Karbala,
a group of my people will kill you, will you are very thirsty. Having
committed such a crime, they will also expect me to vouch for them
on Judgment Day. Allah will not grant them my help, however. My
dear Hussain! Your parents and your brother are with me, and they
are eager to see you. The high levels of heaven awaiting you cannot
be achieved unless through martyrdom...'*

*Imam Hussain (PBUH) prepared to leave Madina. In the dark night,
he visited the graves of his mother and then his brother, bidding them
farewell.*[155]

By visiting the grave of the Holy Prophet (PBUH) two nights in a row, and by
paying pilgrimage to the Holy Prophet's grave, Imam Hussain was making
his final attempts to discover the truth about this incident and find out what
he was to do. As Majlisi has reported, having visited the graves of the Holy
Prophet, Fatima and Imam Hassan – peace be upon them – and prepared to
leave, Imam Hussain (PBUH) saw his brother Muhammad ibn Hanafiyyah,
and the conversation we have already discussed occurred. Imam Hussain
(PBUH) ended his talk with his brother by saying:

> *I have decided to leave for Macca along with my brothers, my nephews
> and my Shiite followers. My decision is their decision, and our views*

---

[155] Muhaddith Qumi, *Nafas ul-Mahmum.*

are the same. You, my brother, however, do not need to leave. Stay in
Madina and keep an eye on what they (i.e. Yazid's men) do. Keep me
posted, and give me every detail.[156]

Imam Hussain wrote the following will and gave it to his brother:

In the Name of Allah, the Compassionate, the Merciful.
This is what Hussain, the son of Ali ibn Abi Talib, has to say to his
brother Muhammad, better known as Muhammad ibn Hanafiyyah.
Hussain acknowledges that there is only one Allah, and Muhammad
was Allah's servant and His appointed prophet. Muhammad
(PBUH) was righteous and rightfully appointed, and heaven and
hell are also true and rightful. There is no doubt that Judgment
Day will come, and on that day, Allah will make all of the dead alive
again. I, Hussain, the son of Ali, have begun this movement neither
to cause wrongdoing, disorder, nor for corruption and oppression. I
have started this uprising only to make reform in and improve my
grandfather Muhammad's people. My aim is to invite people to do
good (and thus bring about their happiness and what is good for
them) and encourage them to avoid evil. I intend to treat the people
the same way my grandfather and Ali ibn Abi Talib did. For those
who accept me as acting on righteousness, I should say that it is
Allah Who deserves to be known as righteous, and for those who
do not accept and acknowledge the uprising and movement I have
started, I shall remain tolerant until Allah judges between me and
these people, for Allah is the best judge of all. My dear brother, this is
my will, and I have submitted it to you. I wish you nothing but the
best from Allah.
Imam Hussain then signed the letter, handed it over to his brother
Muhammad, and left Madina during the night.[157]

The letter presented above leaves no room for any baseless allegations or
covering up of the truth about the goal Hussain (PBUH) was aiming for, was
sacrificing his whole life for, and was taking to the plains and deserts for.
Deceptions, spreading disagreement and conflict, and trampling upon the
clearest of human right are among Machiavellian strategies used by tyrants.
Therefore, in order to eliminate the uproar caused in Islamic societies by the
martyrdom of Imam Hussain (PBUH) Yazid and his men naturally turned
to misinformation and the disruption of realities, attempting to establish
the conclusion that Hussain started his movement with the purpose of
rising to power and taking charge! As a result, Imam Hussain (PBUH)
repeatedly stated the aim of his movement in pleasant, divine words. In
the letter above, which was written in the form of a will addressed to his
brother, Imam Hussain states his faith in Allah, the Holy Prophet (PBUH) as

---

[156] Ibid.
[157] Ibid.

well as acknowledging the righteousness and truth about heaven, hell and Judgment Day, thus verifying and confirming explicitly his belief in Islamic principles so as to eliminate any future suspicion, accusation or allegation about his divine movement. He then presents the supreme goal of his great movement quite clearly:

> I, Hussain, the son of Ali, have been brought up and educated in the school of thought of the Holy Prophet and my father Ali, the son of Abi Talib. My purpose in this uprising is not to bring about evil, cause corruption or disrupt things. I was raised in a family which served to uphold justice, righteousness and other fine human virtues. I have started this uprising in order to reinforce virtues and values and eradicate evils, oppressions and the violations of rights. I have risen to uphold the religion presented by the man Allah chose, Muhammad, the son of Abdullah, who said that even if he were offered the sun in one hand and the moon in the other (i.e. even if he were offered the whole world), he would never give up preaching this religion. My goal and my attitude is the same. I shall do whatever it takes to achieve that goal. It is righteousness which has made me do so. I shall escape no inconvenience or calamity in order to reach that aim. Indeed, true destruction will happen if I fall astray from righteousness and give up defending it rather than upholding what is right and advocating it. If one takes such a path, not only will the obstacles along the way cause one no fear, but in fact triumph will be in one's being torn to pieces while trying to achieve that goal, for one's destination then will ne none other than the destination of the purest and finest descendants of Adam.

Imam Hussain (PBUH) thus leaves for Macca.

> When Hussain (PBUH) left Madina for Macca, Abdullah ibn Muti' saw him and said, 'Where are you heading for, my dear Hussain?'
> 'For now, my destination is Macca,' Imam Hussain replied, 'and then I shall ask Allah to help me determine the best destination for me.'
> 'May Allah have everything go well for you,' Abdullah said. 'When you get to Macca, avoid approaching Kufa, for it is an evil city. That is where your father was killed, and it also the city where the people left your brother all alone, and a sudden attack almost had him killed. Reside in the sacred house of Allah, for you are indeed the master of all Arabs. When they have you, the people of Arabia will never allow anyone else to rule them. Indeed, people will join you from all sides. I beg you, may all of my family be sacrificed for your safety, please avoid the sacred city of Macca. I swear to Allah that if you are martyred, all of us will become slaves.[158]

---

[158] Ibn Al-Athir's *Al-Kamil fil-Tarikh*, Vol. 4.

Abdullah ibn Muti', a distinguished figure of his time, wishes that his life be sacrificed for Imam Hussain (PBUH). He even calls the Imam "the master of all Arabs", which obviously indicates the important role and significant superiority of his character among Muslims. Islam, founded by the Holy Prophet (PBUH), started and spread all over Arabia and then other societies by the Arabs, and as statements made by the Holy Prophet (PBUH) and Imam Ali (PBUH) as well as other significant men of Islamic societies – whether Arab or non-Arab figures – confirm[159], Imam Hussain (PBUH) was indeed the most deserving man worthy of managing the Islamic communities. As Abdullah ibn Muti' has also stated in his above-mentioned words:

> *When they have you, the people of Arabia will never allow anyone else to rule the. Indeed, people will join you from all sides.*

As Shaikh Mufid has quoted from Muhaddith Qumi, who has reported that Imam Sadiq (PBUH) has said:

> *When Imam Hussain (PBUH) decided to leave Macca, a group of angels and a group of jinn proposed to help him, but Imam Hussain (PBUH) did not accept their help.*[160]

The Holy Quran has also pointed out the possibility of assistance from supernatural beings, for example:

> **Remember thou saidst to the Faithful, 'Is it not enough for you that Allah should help you with three thousand angels [specially] sent down?' Indeed, if you remain firm, and act aright, even if the enemy should rush here on you in hot haste, your Lord would help you with five thousand angels, making a terrific onslaught.**[161]

Furthermore:

> **Then Allah sent down His peace upon him, and strengthened him with forces which ye saw not.**[162]

A famous story which shows what a unique character Imam Hussain (PBUH) was occurred when he was on the way to Kufa and saw two men approaching from the city. Imam Hussain (PBUH) dispatched some of his

---

[159] In his *Muqaddimah*, Ibn Khaldun has stated, "Hussain was certain that he was the worthiest and most deserving man to rule, and he was right about that. However, he believed he was able to face Yazid, and that was his mistake." While Ibn Khaldun acknowledges, in Chapter 53 of his work *Muqaddimah*, the fact that the Imams had metaphysical information and were aware of things ordinary people could not know about, Ibn Khaldun has neglected Imam Hussain's goal being concluded by the principle of "one of the two goods".

[160] Ibn Al-Athir's *Al-Kamil fil-Tarikh*, Vol. 4.

[161] The Family of Imran (3:124-125).

[162] Repentance (9:40).

men to ask the two men about the situation in Kufa. "The people we left behind," the two men said, "had their hearts with Hussain, while their swords were ready to kill him."

Indeed, as we all know, cunning, wolf-like politicians can simply confuse and distract the minds of the people in a society and make them pick up their swords and confront a man for whom their hearts have compassion and love, thus creating a battle between people and the man who is their favorite!

Part 19

Did Imam Hussain (PBUH) Know that He Would Be Martyred in This Great Uprising?

Several theories have been posed in order to answer this question, and extensive discussions and studies have also been devoted to the issue. We shall consider two of the prominent theories here:

Theory 1: Although Imam Hussain's uprising was by all means righteous, correct and motivated by the duty Allah had given him, he did not know he would be martyred in battle. In his *Muqaddimah*, Ibn Khaldun has implied, as several other thinkers have as well, that Imam Hussain (PBUH) was not aware of the fact that he would be killed in Iraq. However, this point of view of Ibn Khaldun's is in conflict with the footnote presented in our previous chapter. As for others who believe Imam Hussain (PBUH) did not know that he was going to be martyred, reasons will be provided below, when we discuss the second theory.

Theory 2: Imam Hussain (PBUH) knew that he would be martyred. This theory has been studied along with various explanations in accounts and treatises of the Karbala event. Let us take this important issue into further consideration:

1. Imams were supernatural leaders, and their Allah-given supreme stance allowed them to enjoy intuitive knowledge of the future and the unseen.

2. As stated in the Holy Quran (The Jinn 72:26-27):

   He (alone) knows the Unseen, nor does He make any one acquainted with His Mysteries, except an apostle whom He has chosen.

The above verse explicitly states that beings other than Allah can also have supernatural knowledge. Thus, if Allah's Will makes it happen, others can also be informed of supernatural happenings. Many verses have stated that the Holy Prophet (PBUH) received supernatural knowledge thanks to revelations from Allah, and the Imams acquired it from the Holy prophet.[163]

3. Having pointed out cases of Imam Jafar Sadiq (PBUH) knowing about the unseen, Chapter 53 of Ibn Khaldun's *Muqaddimah* reads:

   If the blessing of intuitive knowledge of the unseen and supernatural discovery is possible for other people (i.e. those human beings who

---

[163] See Allamah Tabatabai's interpretation of the two verses mentioned here (The Jinn 72:26-27) in his work *Tafsir-e Al-Mizan*.

have gone through austerity and have succeeded in purifying their
soul and controlling their desires and whims), the family of the Holy
Prophet, who are quite pure and chaste when it comes to knowledge,
religion and divine blessings, are even more deserving when it comes
to being capable of receiving supernatural knowledge.

4. The Holy Prophet (PBUH) has also been reported to have foreseen many things in the future, such as a detailed account of how Imam Ali (PBUH) would be murdered.[164]

Cases of Imam Ali's Supernatural Knowledge of Events

Ibn Abi l-Hadid has written:[165]

In this chapter, we shall go through things which Imam Ali had
supernatural knowledge of and had said that they would occur, and
they really did happen later on.
Beware that Imam Ali has sworn to Allah, Who has control of his
life, that the people will not ask about any event from now until
Judgment Day that has not already been foreseen by Imam Ali, such
as a clan which will lead a hundred people to the right path, another
hundred people who will fall into the wrong path, news about leaders,
preachers, riders, where they will get off their horses, which people
will be killed, and those who will die natural deaths.

Imam Ali (PBUH) has not claimed to be Allah or the Prophet here; he has merely stated that he received information about these events from the Holy Prophet (PBUH). Having studied the predictions made by Imam Ali (PBUH) and compared them with realities and real events, we found all of the Imam's statements to prove to have come true. Thus, it can be concluded that his claim was quite honest and truthful. Here are a few examples:

1. Imam Ali had foretold that he would be struck on the head, and the blood from his head would make his beard look all red.
2. His prediction regarding Imam Hussain's getting killed.
3. While passing through Karbala toward Siffin, Imam Ali (PBUH) predicted what would happen there later on and how Imam Hussain (PBUH) would be martyred there.
4. He had predicted that Mu'awiyah would rise to power after Imam Ali's death.
5. He had described Mu'awiyah and his command to insult Imam Ali (PBUH).

---

[164] Abu Na'im Al-Isfahani, *Dala'il al-Nubuwwa* (*"The Signs and Proofs of Prophethood"*). Also see Al-Suyuti, Jalaliddin, *Al-Jaami' al-Saghir*, Vol. 1, as quoted from Abu Na'im Al-Isfahani's *Hilyat al-Awliya'*.

[165] See Jafari, Muhammad Taqi, *A Translation and Interpretation of the Nahjulbalaghah*, Vol. 16.

6. His predictions regarding Hajjaj ibn Yusuf.[166]
7. His predictions regarding Yusuf ibn Umar.[167]
8. His predictions about the Mariqin (those of the Khawarij who battled Imam Ali in the Battle of Nahrawan).
9. His predictions about those of the Khawarij who would be killed and those who would be hanged.
10. His predictions about Talhah and Zubayr ("The Nakithin") and their followers, who started the Battle of the Camel.
11. His predictions about Mu'awiyah and Amr ibn Al-As ("The Qasitin"[168]) and their gangs.
12. About to leave for Basra in order to battle the "Allies of the Battle of the Camel"[169], Imam Ali (PBUH) had foreseen the number of troops moving out from Kufa against him.
13. In regard to Abdullah ibn Zubayr, Imam Ali (PBUH) said, "He will not achieve what he wants. He uses religion as a rope [i.e. as a bait] to hunt this world." [Imam Ali (PBUH) described him as "a deceiving, vengeful man who would fail to accomplish what he desired. Moreover, he will be hanged by the Quraysh."]
14. Imam Ali (PBUH) had predicted that Basra would be drowned and a great loss of life would occur.
15. Imam Ali (PBUH) had also predicted the many killings in Basra due to the Zanj Rebellion, which was led by a man known as Ali ibn Muhammad ibn Ahmad ibn Issa ibn Zaid.
16. He had predicted the rising of black flags from Khurasan, and that peoples from that area known as Bani Raziq would be involved in the movement. They were of Mus'ab's clan including Tahir ibn Al-Hussain as well as his son Ishaq ibn Ibrahim, who were all supporters of the Abbasids.
17. Imam Ali had predicted that some of his offspring would later emerge as leaders in lands suck as Tabaristan, Hassan ibn Ali Al-Nasir and Al-Da'i[170] for instance. He had said:

> *Muhammad's clan have a treasury in Taliqan, which will arise if Allah wills it to. His preaching will be righteous. He*

---

[166] Abu Muhammad Al-Hajjaj ibn Yusuf ibn Al-Hakam ibn Aqil Al-Thaqafi (661-714) was a notable governor in the Umayyad Caliphate. [Translator]

[167] Yusuf ibn Umar al-Thaqafi was a senior provincial governor for the Umayyad Caliphate. [Translator]

[168] Those who pledged allegiance to Mu'awiyah and fought Imam Hussain (PBUH). [Translator]

[169] Ayashah, Talhah and Zubayr, who fought Imam Ali (PBUH) in the Battle of the Camel. [Translator]

[170] Al-Hassan ibn Zayd ibn Muhammad ibn Isma'il ibn al-Hasan ibn Zayd (died 884), also known as *al-Da'i al-kabir* ("the Great/Elder Missionary"), was an a descendent of Imam Ali's who became the founder of the Zaydid dynasty of Tabaristan. [Translator]

will rise on Allah's command and invite people to join Allah's religion.

18. He had predicted that Muhammad al-Nafs al-Zakiyya[171] would be killed beside the dark stones in Madina.

19. He had predicted that Ibrahim, the brother of Muhammad al-Nafs al-Zakiyya, would be killed at the "Hamzah" entrance.

    He will be killed after he rises, and he will be defeated after he defeats.

20. Imam Ali (PBUH) has also made predictions regarding how Ibrahim would die:

    He will be struck by an arrow, but the archer will not be found. That arrow will be Ibrahim's death. May that archer be damned; may his arms and his hands grow weak.

21. He has been reported to have made predictions regarding those killed in Waj (Ta'if, where the Holy Prophet did his last battle, was known as Waj); of course, this is definitely a mistake, for the correct name is Fakh[172], whose residents were described by Imam Ali (PBUH) as the best people on earth.

22. Imam Ali (PBUH) had foreseen the Alavid government that would be established in the West. He had even mentioned the name Kitama, the men who helped Abu Abdullah Al-Da'i Mu'allim.

23. He had also made predictions about Abu Abdullah Al-Mahdi, a man of noble birth who was the governor of Qairawan. Moreover, Imam Ali (PBUH) also made predictions regarding Ubaidullah ibn Al-Mahdi, a slightly chubby man with fair complexions and soft muscles. It had been predicted that Ismail ibn Jafar ibn Muhammad would be laid in a robe. In fact, when Ismail died, his father wrapped him in a robe and laid him there for the Shiite elite to see that he was dead.

24. In regard to the Bani Buwaih clan, Imam Ali (PBUH) had predicted that a clan would arise from Banu al-Sayyad Dailaman, referring to the Bani Buwaih. The grandfather of the clan would catch fish with his bare hands and sell the fish to take care of his family. From his offspring, Allah would create three kings, and their generation would become so widespread that their kingdom became an exemplary figure. Imam Ali (PBUH) added that they would even take over Zawra' (now known as Baghdad) and overthrow the

---

[171] Muhammad ibn Abdullah ibn al-Hasan al-Muthanna ibn al-Hasan al-Mujtaba ibn 'Ali ibn Abi Talib, also known as Muhammad al-Nafs al-Zakiyya ("The Pure Soul"), was a descendant of the Holy Prophet (PBUH) through his daughter Fatimah (PBUH). [Translator]

[172] Fakh is a location near Macca. On the 16th of Thil-Hijja, 169 Hijra, which was later known as "Fakh Day", many Alavids were killed here. [Translator]

caliphs. When asked how long their rule would last, Imam Ali (PBUH) replied, "A hundred, more or less."

25. He had foreseen that Mutrif ibn Ajzam, from the Bani Buwaih clan, would be murdered by his cousin by the Tigris. Imam Ali (PBUH) was in fact referring to Izzuddawlah Bakhtiar ibn Mu'izzuddawlah Abul Hassan. Mu'izzuddawlah's hand had been cut off due to the crime he had committed. Imam Ali (PBUH) had also predicted that he would overthrow caliphs; indeed, he ousted Al-Mustakfi Billah and appointed Al-Muti'ullah in his stead. He also ousted Baha'uddowlah Abu Nasr ibn Azududdawlah Al-Ta'i and appointed Al-Qadir to succeed him. The duration of their rule was also in accordance with Imam Ali's predictions.

26. He had told Abdullah ibn Abbas that his offspring would rise to power.

> When Ali ibn Abdullah was born, his father brought him before Imam Ali (PBUH). Imam Ali (PBUH) put some of his saliva into the baby's mouth, and then fastened the baby's chin using some palm dates he had been chewing. Then Imam Ali (PBUH) handed the baby back to his father and said, 'Take this, O father of kings.'

This was the accurate account of what had happened. Abul Abbas Mubarrad has also reported this story in his book *Al-Kamil*, but his account of the number of Abdullah ibn Abbas's children is incorrect. There have been many cases in which Imam Ali (PBUH) has accurately foreseen events similar to those mentioned here, and a thorough study of them would prove quite voluminous. Biographies have provided detailed explanations regarding such predictions.[173]

27. Imam Ali (PBUH) had foreseen the situations awaiting him and events that would happen to him later on.

28. He had foreseen the tense events that were to occur in Kufa later on.

29. He had talked about Marwan ibn Hakam and his offspring, who would bring about a bloody day for the Islamic nation.

30. Imam Ali (PBUH) had foretold that the Bani Umayyads would rise to power for a short period of time, but then lose whatever they had come to gain.

31. Imam Ali (PBUH) had spoken of a misled man in Damascus who would do a lot of shouting and have his flags raised on the outskirts of Kufa.

32. Foreseeing the invasions of the Mongolians and the killings and ravaging that would be brought about by them.

33. There are countless instances of the Holy Prophet and Imam Ali having been reported to have foreseen Imam Hussain's martyrdom in various Shiite and Sunni books. The number of writers who have

---

[173] Ibn Abi al-Hadid, *Sharh Nahjulbalaghah*, Vol. 7.

quoted these predictions is so high that whoever is not convinced will probably not be convinced by anything at all. Here are several examples of these sources:

- *Kamil al-Ziyarat*, by Ibn Qawlawayh
- *Ihqaq ul-Haq*, by Nurullah Shushtari
- *Amali*, by Shaikh Tusi, quoted from *Tarikh ul-Khamis*
- *Bihar ul-Anwar*, by Allamah Majlisi
- *Yanabi ul-Mawaddah*, by Sulayman Al-Qunduzi
- *Mawdah al-Qurba*, by Sayyid Ali Hamadani
- *Al-Mu'jam ul-Kabir*, by Al-Tabarani
- *Tahdhib al-Tahdhib* by Ibn Hajar Al-Asqalani
- *Al-Fusul Al-Muhimmah*, by Ibn Sabaq Maliki
- *Maqtal al-Husayn*, by Khawarazmi
- *Maqtal al-'Awalim*, by Abdullah Nur-Allah al-Bahrani
- *Al Khasais-ul-Kubra*, by Jalaluddin Al-Suyuti
- *Kifayat ul-Talib fi Manaqib Ali ibn Abi Talib*, by Muhammad ibn Yusuf Ganji Shafi'i
- *Majma' al-Zawa'id*, by Al-Haithami
- *Kanz al-Ummal* *("Treasure of the Doers of Good Deeds")*, by Ala'iddin Ali ibn Abd-al-Malik Husamuddin al-Muttaqi al-Hindi
- *Kitab al-Irshad*, by Al-Mufid
- *Al-Bidayah Wan-Nihayah* *("The Beginning and the End")*, by Ibn Kathir
- Ahmad ibn Hanbal's *Musnad*
- *Tarikh Atham Kufi*, by Ahmad ibn Atham al-Kufi
- *Qamus al-Rijal*, Vol. 1, by Muhammad Taqi Shushtari
- *Luhuf*, by Sayyid ibn Tawus
- *Kashf al-Ghumma fi Ma'rifat al-A'imma* ("Lifting the Hardship in Knowing the Leaders") by Baha'uddin Ali ibn 'Isa al-Irbili
- *Wafa al-Wafa bi Akhbar Dar al-Mustafa*, by Ali bin Ahmad al-Samhudi
- *Tabaqat*, by Ibn Sa'd
- *al-Sawa'iq al-Muhriqah*, by Ibn Hajar Al-Asqalani
- *Zakhair ul-Uqba* by Muhib al-Tabari
- *Tathkarat ul-Khawas*, by Sibt ibn Al-Jawzi
- *Usd al-Ghabah fi Ma'rifat al-Sahabah* *("The Lions of the Forest and the knowledge about the Companions")*, by Ibn Al-Athir
- *Nur Ul Absar Fi Manaqib Al Nabi Al Mukhtar*, by Mu'min ibn Hassan Shablanji
- *Al-Akhbar Al-Tiwal* *("General History")*, by Abu Hanifah Ahmad ibn Dawud Dinwari
- *Hayat -ul- Hayawan*, Vol. 1, by Shaykh Kamaluddin Al-Damiri
- *As-Sirat un-Nabawiyyah* *("The Biography of the Prophet")*, Vol. 3, by Ibn Hisham

- *Sharh Nahjulbalaghah,* Vol. 2., by Ibn Abi al-Hadid

Two questions arise regarding this theory (about Imam Hussain's being martyred):

Question 1: Does awareness that one is to be killed in an event mean that one is allowed to take action and decide to take part in the event? Those who make no distinction between people and see all events as equal – and see an ordinary death as no different from being martyred in order to defend lives and virtues necessary for man's physical and spiritual life – believe that life is the absolute desired thing in the realm of being, and nothing can be as desirable as life. Therefore, if one knows that one is to be killed in an event, one's participation in such an event will be regarded as illegal when it comes to standards of canonical laws and reason. Considering the immense importance of life, even if there is a potential danger, one must not take any action in such events, let alone when there is certainty of fatality. In order to answer this question, we must first gain accurate knowledge of the meaning of life when it is described as "the absolute desired in the realm of being".

Indeed, what is the meaning of life, the absolute desired thing in the universe and the realm of being? If "life" only means eating, drinking and fulfilling one's purely natural instincts, there is no doubt that those who consider the truth of life lying in spiritual greatness, metaphysical virtues and divine perfection – the best reasons why life is eternal – will not see life as an absolutely animal-like phenomenon. In fact, considering the myriad of inconveniences, hardships and deprivations such a life involves, they will actually see it as bitter, and going on with such a life will have to be the result of a kind of necessity and the need to reinforce the foundations of life. Of course, this does not mean that such a phenomenon is innately and absolutely desirable. If we take into consideration all of the acts of suicide and those people who have seriously wished to die when intolerable suffering comes upon them – throughout history and in nations all over the world – we will come across one of the clearest reasons why a purely animal-like life cannot be the absolutely desirable one.

If by life we are referring to "intelligible life" (a kind of life based on reason and intelligibility, a life which belongs to Allah and flows for Allah)[174], the animal-like life mentioned above will not only fail to be the absolutely desired life, but it will also disrupt "intelligible life", which deserves to reach Allah's rays of Divine Attraction. Of course, those who know nothing about

---

[174] The term "intelligible life" has been based on three descriptions of true life in the Holy Quran:

a) "Whoever works righteousness, man or woman, and has Faith, verily, to him We will give a new Life, a life that is good and pure. (The Bee 16:97)

b) "… that those who died might die after a clear Sign [had been given], and those who lived might live after a Clear Sign [had been given]. " (Spoils of War 8:42)

c) "Say: Truly, my prayer and my service of sacrifice, my life and my death, are [all] for Allah, the Cherisher of the Worlds. " (Cattle 6:162)

intelligible life and life based on divine principles, or those who do know but fail to follow that lifestyle because they are weak or cannot avoid animal desires, see animal-like natural life as indeed the greatest ideal possible and devote all of their capabilities into achieving it.

In short, for those who see life in an intelligible life – which originates from Allah's wisdom and eternal blessings and continues up to being in Allah's presence – purely natural life is a useful means to reach intelligible life, and conscious human beings will be willing to lose their purely natural life a thousand times if it means achieving intelligible life in return. This immense feeling is reported to have been experienced by Imam Hussain's loyal, conscious companions on the night before Ashura. As for those who cast doubt upon the greatness of sacrifice and getting killed in the path of *jihad* and as an effort to defend people's lives, honor, dignity, and intelligible human virtues, we have nothing to say to such selfish advocates of sophistry. We are addressing those who see human life as something beyond eating, drinking, fulfilling their lusts; those who see life as higher than "I am the end and others are the means" and regard it with a supreme notion instead. Obviously, defense and *jihad* means moving along the borders of life and death. By studying the ideas of great figures of the history of mankind and the most mature-minded human beings humanity has seen, we shall see that these fine people preferred death to a life of humiliation, confinement, animal lusts, and disgrace. As Imam Hussain (PBUH) said in Dhi-Hussum when facing Kufa:

> *I see death as prosperity and emancipation, for living alongside oppressors and wrongdoers involves nothing but anxiety, sorrow and frustration.*[175]

There is a truth that literary cultures of various peoples and nations in the world have frequently pointed out: **A red death is better than a life of disgrace, humiliation and shame.**

The truth is that by observing one supreme truth about life, this life can become quite easy to tolerate, interpret and justify:

> *We are quite passionate for our host, who is also our hunter;*
> *otherwise, this cage can be broken with even a half-cry...*

Moreover, we are all aware that:

> *Time, and the passing of days would be in fact a mere plaything*
> *if the long day of this world were to have no tomorrow...*

Therefore, it is only belief in eternity and the supreme philosophy of our

---

[175] Muhaddith Qumi, *Nafas ul-Mahmum.*

being that makes the world and time not seem like a plaything.[176] By logically and correctly perceiving this truth, dignified, conscious, honest human beings can prepare to answer the six basic questions (Who am I? Where have I come from? Where am I now? Who am I with? Why have I come? Where do I go from here?) and achieve an intelligible life.

Question 2: How can one's awareness of being killed in an event prove to be compatible with one's activities and thoughts regarding that event and one's achievement of one's goal in it? In other words, when someone knows he will be killed in the course of an event, how could he take action in order to achieve his goal and think about accomplishment in such an event? Now let us suppose that Imam Hussain (PBUH) indeed knew that he would be martyred in the Karbala event. With that in mind, and considering his goal – establishing a government of justice in the Islamic society – how could he leave his residence in Macca, having taken a great deal of care and regarded the letters of invitation he had received from Kufa as well as having dispatched Muslim ibn Aqil beforehand in order to provide the grounds, and set off along with his army of 72 men? To answer this question, we will first have to make a concise study of how well human beings understand life and death in order to be able to better discuss the issue of Imam Hussain's knowledge of his eventual martyrdom.

---

[176] This is a fact all wise, conscientious scientists and scholars of both the East and the West are in agreement on. For example, as Barthélemy-Saint-Hilaire has clearly stated in his foreword to Aristotle's *Nicomachean Ethics*, "Unless we accept that there is an eternity behind this world, this life will remain an unsolvable mystery."

Moreover, we read in *The Garden of Epicurus,* by Anatole France, that: "It is the power and charity of religions which teaches man about the existence of being and the consequences of man's actions. When we abolish the principles of the belief of divine philosophy – as almost all of us do so in this era of science and freedom – there is no other means for us to find out why we have come to this world. The secret of fate has surrounded all of us by means of its powerful mysteries, and we should truly think of nothing at all if we are to avoid feeling the sad ambiguity of life. The roots of our sorrow and sadness lie in our absolute ignorance about the reason for our being. Our spiritual and physical pains, the sufferings our souls go through, the happiness felt by the decadent and the pains suffered by the honest would all become tolerable again if we were to discover their philosophies, if we could believe in a divine will. The faithful enjoy the tortures and mental suffering they undergo, and the injustices and hardships their enemies afflict upon them [of course, when they are unable to defend themselves] prove delightful and pleasant for them. Even when they commit sins or do wrong, they do not lose hope. However, in a world where the flames of faith have gone out, even pain and disease lose their meanings, and are regarded as nothing but wicked jokes and evil acts of ridicule."

Part 20

Human Beings Greatly Differ in Their Understanding of Life and Death and the Truth about Life and Death

There is no doubt that human beings are in a period of absolute life as of their childhood, even though they do not even know what life means. Naturally, during this period, they have no perception of death either; they are like a fish in the sea – a fish has no idea how it will feel once it is thrown out of the water!

Gradually, however, as human beings grow older and see and hear about others dying, they encounter the phenomenon of death, albeit with some vagueness.

Having understood that their life ends with death, people experience a variety of attitudes and mindsets in regard to life and death.

1. Some people become so engulfed and immersed in the aspects of purely natural life that they continue the same state of mind they had in childhood. These people never contemplate death or attempt to interpret life coming to an end due to death. Sometimes people are so engulfed by life that even though they know that their lives will come to an end – as everyone's life will – they still ignore this fact. It is obvious that they avoid remembering death and avoid thinking about the afterworld through various ways of inculcations which are sometimes so ridiculous that people feel ashamed to even express them. They also assume that their lives will never be destroyed; from their point of view, "death is only for others!"

2. Sometimes people are not too drowned in their purely natural lives to avoid ignoring death, but the sweetness of life and its pleasures make death disappear from man's life, as if there is no certainty about death! As Imam Ali (PBUH) once said, "Some people's certainty toward death is in fact doubt." Indeed, death has become too distant from the scope of such people's minds.

3. Some people feel certain about death, but due to the doubts they have regarding the world of afterlife, they cannot adjust and justify their lives so that death and the afterlife can cast an effective light upon them.

The three groups of people mentioned above have one thing in common – they have a vague life. They often live in the present – neither the past nor the future is of any concern to them, unless it directly pertains to now. In other words, their lives are like detached links of a chain, passing by.

Therefore, such people are not concerned with a truth known as life which can be interpreted and justified within the universe; nor are they concerned with death as a complementary part of life. Nevertheless, even if the three groups of people mentioned above, due to various reasons, do take death into consideration, theirs will be an attitude of sorrow and anxiety. Avicenna has studied the factors bringing about such sadness and anxiety in a special book, *Risalatun fi Daf'il Ghamm min Al-mawt* (*"A Book on How to Avoid the Sadness about Dying"*).

Considering the existing differences among people's perceptions of life and death, there are also other groups which we shall not discuss here. All of them have one thing in common – their lack of knowledge regarding life; the following verse of the Holy Quran is applicable to all of them:

> *They know but the outer [things] in the life of this world, but of the End of things [i.e. the afterworld] they are heedless.*[177]

Unfortunately, they even go so far as stating things based on their incomplete knowledge and calling it the humanities!

---

[177] Rome (30:7)

Part 21

An Introduction to How to Understand the Compatibility of Knowing about Martyrdom or Efforts toward a Lawful Life

With the Enhancement of the Human Character, two Significant Truths about Life and Death Revealed to Man:

The First Truth: Life and death are complementary parts of the orderly universe.

It is obvious that life is not a scattered, disheveled phenomenon free of all constraints; life cannot be considered as being in an isolated vacuum. Every phenomenon is a part of the set of realities in the universe, and it is impossible to attain sufficient or necessary knowledge of the phenomenon without gaining general knowledge of the whole, albeit in brief. Likewise, it is impossible to achieve true knowledge of a component related to other parts of the whole without first attaining knowledge of the other components, whether collectively or individually.

Thus, to understand the truth about life, it is essential for us to have general knowledge about the basic principles regarding this immense cosmos, of which the phenomenon known as life is a highly significant part of.

Having achieved such knowledge, we shall see that life and death are two complementary components of this vast universe. Thus, those human beings who have well-matured, developed minds know that one should look far beyond death; the phenomenon known as death is by no means voidance, annihilation or oblivion. For such wise people, it is a fact that life is a truth created by Allah's will; life passes through the laws and materials of the cosmos, and for some time, it resides within human beings, cultivating and developing their "selves" (i.e. their egos), thus preparing them to cross over the bridge of death and pass on to their eternal homes.

The Second Truth: As man's character develops and matures, man discovers that although this life seems to be a continuing unit, it is in fact made of a flow of continual parts, like the particles light consists of. Let us consider the following verses of Rumi's:

> The world is always renewing and refreshing itself; yet, we are still in silence and stagnancy.
> Our life is flowing by like the drops of water in a river, even though

> *they may seem constant and motionless in the human body.*[178]

Furthermore:

> *Why are we unable to comprehend the motion of existence and*
> *voidance?*
> *When you make a bowl of burning charcoal rotate, for example,*
> *you see a real circle form, but it is in fact not a real circle.*
> *It is the quick movement of the bowl which makes it look like a circle.*
> *Also, throw a burning twig in a direct line, and you will see a line*
> *of fire.*
> *Thus, you will assume the lengthy continuation of matter as a true*
> *entity.*
> *If you look carefully, you will see that you are existent and void in*
> *every moment of your life.*
> *As the Holy Prophet put it, "The world is but one moment."*[179]

Considering the principle of the continuance of Allah's blessing and kindness for the survival of creatures, particularly regarding the phenomenon of life, the importance of this truth is quite clear. Moreover, the following renowned *hadith* from Imam Hassan Mujtaba and Imam Hussain (PBUH) also provide useful clarification:

> **Regarding this world, act like you are going to live forever; as**
> **for the afterworld, on the other hand, act like you are going to**
> **die tomorrow.**[180]

Having understood the above truth, we realize that the character of human beings of well-matured, developed minds always fluctuate between the borders of the natural and the supernatural (i.e. life and beyond life). This form of life goes beyond ordinary life; while taking into consideration the factors and requirements of ordinary life, it also intuitively considers the needs and consequences of life coming to an end. In fact, every moment of such a life is both the path and the destination – in other words, both the means and the end. This form of life is based on the principle of achieving "one of the two goods" ("*Ihda-al-Husnayain*"), which involves both a life of emancipation and a death of emancipation. As the Holy Quran has stated:

> **Truly, my prayer and my service of sacrifice, my life and my**
> **death, are [all] for Allah, the Cherisher of the Worlds.**[181]

It is obvious that living an ordinary life in which the goal is likely to be achieved is the first "good" and prioritized over martyrdom, which is the second "good".

---

[178] Rumi's *Mathnawi*, Book 1.

[179] Ibid.

[180] Allamah Majlisi, Muhammad Baqir, *Bihar ul-Anwar*, Vol. 44.

[181] The Cattle (6:162)

Thus, Imam Hussain (PBUH) knew very well that he would be martyred and that martyrdom is one of the two forms of emancipation. Based on such a sense of duty, he chose this path of life; this was what he needed to do. It was as though every moment of this life – which was soon to come to an end – was en eternal life, and a well-developed human being should make the most of this chance to achieve emancipation. There is, however, a highly significant point which needs to be noted here:

A mature-minded human being's knowledge of his or her survival at a certain time or of his or her death or martyrdom at a certain time is not the form of absolute knowledge which is exclusive to Allah alone.

As we have already discussed, prophets, Imams, and even some pure, great men of Allah, due to the fact that they have refined and purified their souls by adhering to divine moral ethics, are able to understand things naturally unseen, such as the end of life (whether death or martyrdom). Nevertheless, this is not absolute knowledge; it is not what Islamic sources see as equivalent to the treasure of knowledge kept by Allah. Therefore, the Imams may have known about their being martyred at a certain time due to the knowledge their position as Imams bestowed upon them, but the degree and extent of this knowledge could never reach Allah's knowledge; as the Holy Quran states:

> *Allah doth blot out or confirm what He pleaseth: with Him is the Mother of the Book.*[182]

It is this very possibility of events superior to and beyond the knowledge of Imams that makes it necessary for them to fulfill all of the decisions and actions in their lives.

This was a detailed study of the following issues:

1. Did Imam Hussain (PBUH) know that he would be martyred in this great uprising?
2. The predictions the Holy Prophet (PBUH) had made.
3. Two questions can be posed about the theory of Imam Hussain's knowledge of his own martyrdom:
   a. If someone knows that he will be killed in an incident, is it still legitimate and rightful to decide to get involved in such an incident?
   b. How can knowledge of one's being killed in an incident be compatible with the goals, thoughts and actions in one's life?
4. An introduction on how to understand that knowing that one will be martyred can be in conformity with one's endeavors in everyday life. As the human character develops, two important truths regarding life and death need to be taken into consideration:

The First Truth: Life and death are two complementary components in the

---

[182] Thunder (13:39).

orderly universe.

The Second Truth: Although life appears to be a continuous unit, it is in fact a flow made of separate parts, as is light.

5. The knowledge of a mature-minded human being about his survival at a certain time or his death or martyrdom at a certain time is not equivalent to the absolute knowledge which is exclusive to Allah. This very well proves that Imam Hussain (PBUH) may have known that he was going to be martyred in the Karbala event, just as Imam Ali (PBUH) was aware that he was going to be assaulted on the 19th of Ramadan. Ultimately, however, it is not the same as the absolute treasure of knowledge Allah possesses. Thus, the reasons and evidence pertaining to Imam Hussain's knowing about his martyrdom at Karbala are no longer ignored. In fact, his movement will always be the best model and example for human beings who feel obliged to make efforts for the betterment of their society. Now let us return to Imam Hussain's departure toward Macca.

As he was leaving for Macca, Imam Hussain (PBUH) recited the following verse of the Holy Quran:

> *He therefore got away therefrom, looking about, in a state of fear. He prayed "O my Lord! Save me from people given to wrong-doing.*[183]

The above verse regards Moses (PBUH), who was feeling quite anxious and fearful that bad events were going to happen when he had left Egypt, and asked Allah to save him from the wrongdoing.

Imam Hussain (PBUH) took the main road. His family suggested that he should take a different path (which would be safer), but he disagreed. "No," he told them, "I swear to Allah that we shall take this road, and see what Allah has in store for us."

As we have already mentioned, Imam Hussain's natural life was in line with the laws of life. Therefore, when he went to see Walid ibn Utbah, he took along with him members of his family so that they could come to his defense of his life was at peril. Some might say that if Imam Hussain (PBUH) knew that he was going to be martyred in Karbala, he should not have recited that verse on the way to Macca. In response, we must say that Imam Hussain (PBUH) was in fact implying all of the events from his departure from Madina to the end of the uprising. In other words, in those events and until the events were over, he saw his lawful, legal life – which is the "first good" (divine happiness and prosperity) if he began his uprising as an effort to establish a government of justice and righteousness – endangered by inhuman wrongdoers, for Allah's knowledge is superior to the knowledge an Imam is endowed with, and anything was possible. Although losing his life (i.e. martyrdom) was desirable for Hussain (PBUH), it is obvious that achieving success in his movement in his life was a higher priority.

---

[183] Narration (28:21).

Given the fact that Hussain (PBUH) used any means he could in order to defend his own life as well as the lives of his family and his friends, it is clear that he knew quite well that he would have faced no danger if he had taken an ordinary road, and if he were to face any danger, it would have been due to reasons beyond his knowledge as Imam – reasons arising from Allah's treasury of absolute knowledge.

Three days into Sh'aban month, the night before a Friday, Imam Hussain (PBUH) arrived in Macca, reciting the following verse of the Holy Quran:

> **Then, when he [Moses] turned his face towards [the land of] Madyan, he said, 'I do hope that my Lord will show me the smooth and straight Path.'**[184]

Reciting the above-mentioned verse, like the repetition of the verses, "*Thee do we worship, and Thine aid we seek. Show us the straight way,*"[185] in Muslims' everyday prayers, clearly shows that even Muhammad ibn Abdullah, the last of the Prophets and the infallible Imams (may peace be upon all of them) require help from Allah in every moment of their lives.

> *The people of Macca, and also people from other places and other lands who had come for pilgrimage, poured in to see Imam Hussain. Abdullah ibn Zubayr, who was in Macca, blended in with the groups of people who came to visit Imam Hussain (PBUH). Sometimes he would do so two days in a row, or every other day. At this time, Hussain's existence was the heaviest burden in the world for the son of Zubayr, for he knew very well that the people would not take his side as long as Hussain was there. Indeed, the people saw Hussain as a much greater man, a man who deserved to be followed and obeyed.*[186]

The people of Kufa, having learned that Mu'awiyah was dead, were intensely anxious about Yazid's rise to power. They heard that Imam Hussain (PBUH) had refused to make a pledge of allegiance with Yazid had moved to Macca. They had also learned that Ibn Zubayr had also refused to make a pledge of allegiance with Yazid and had moved to Macca. Shiites gathered at Sulaiman ibn Surad's house, telling him about Mu'awiyah's death and praising Allah. "Mu'awiyah is dead, and Hussain has moved to Macca," Sulaiman told them, "and you are Shiites following Hussain and his father. If you are truly certain that you intend to help Hussain and fight his enemy, write to him and inform him that you plan to aid him. If you are afraid that you might not feel strong enough to do so, and that your unity might break apart, do not deceive him." "We will help him," they all said. "We shall put all of our efforts into defending him, and we will even put our lives on the line." "If

---

[184] Narration (28:22).

[185] The Opening Chapter (1:4-5).

[186] Ibn Al-Athir, *Al-Kamil fil-Tarikh*, Vol. 4, despite the slight differences compared to the account presented by Muhaddith Qumi.

that is so," Sulaiman said, "then write to him." The people of Kufa then wrote many letters to Imam Hussain (PBUH):

> *In the Name of Allah, the Compassionate, the Merciful.*
> *This is a letter from Sulaiman ibn Surad, Musayyib ibn Najiyyah Fazari, Rafa'at ibn Shaddad and Habib ibn Mazahir as well as other Shiites following Hussain and the faithful and the Muslims in Kufa to Hussain, the son of Ali. Praise be to Allah, Who defeated your stubborn, wrongdoing enemy. The enemy who dominated the people, deprived them of the basics of their lives, appropriated their treasury, ruled over them without their consent, killed the finest human beings among the people, opened the doors of evil, and allowed Allah's possessions to be used by oppressors and wealthy despotic figures. May they fall far from Allah's blessings, as the Thamud were abolished from Allah's blessings. At the moment, we have no one to lead us. Please come over to us, may Allah guide us toward the right path through your help. Nu'man ibn Bashir is in the governor's palace, but we shall neither say Friday prayers with him nor accompany him on religious celebrations. If we learn that you are coming to join us, we shall remove him from power and, with Allah's help, we shall send him back to Damascus [to his master].*

Then, they had Ubaidullah ibn Musamma' Hamdani and Abdullah ibn Wal Tamimi deliver the letter to Imam Hussain (PBUH). The two men were ordered to make their trip fast. On the tenth of Ramadan, they reached Imam Hussain (PBUH) in Macca and handed him the letter. Two days later, the people of Kufa sent Imam Hussain (PBUH) 150 pages of letters including numerous signatures. And two days after that, they had Hani ibn Hani Sabee'ee and Sa'id ibn Abdullah Hanafi deliver yet another to Imam Hussain (PBUH). The letter read:

> *In the Name of Allah, the Compassionate, the Merciful.*
> *This is a letter from the Shiites and the faithful following Hussain, the son of Ali. Praise be to Allah and peace be upon the Holy Prophet. Please come here quickly, for the people are waiting for you, and they are thinking of no one else but you. Please hasten your departure, and hurry over to us, may Allah bless you.*
> *Shabath ibn Raba'ee, Hajjar ibn Abjar Ajali, Yazid ibn Harith ibn Ruyam Shaibani, Amr ibn Qeys Ahmasi, Amr ibn Hajjaj Zubaidi, and Muhammad ibn Amr Tamimi have also written:*
> *Praise be to Allah, and peace be upon the Holy Prophet. Our city is green and beautiful now; the fruits are ripe. If you decide to come to us, you shall find our combat-ready troops at your service. May*

peace be with you.[187]

*   *   *

All of the men who had brought letters gathered at Imam Hussain's house. He read the letters and asked about the state the people were in. Then Imam Hussain said prayers, asking Allah to show him the best way for him.[188]

The reason why the people of Kufa were anxious having heard about Yazid's rise to power after Mu'awiyah's death was the many oppressions and frequent violations they had seen Mu'awiyah commit. The animosity the Umayyids had toward followers of Ali ibn Abi Talib or anyone who was likely to have contact with the Holy Prophet's infallible clan is one of the most shameful truths in history, which shows how man can confront righteousness and good in return for the pleasures of power and wealth and the chance to commit any wrongdoing or tyranny he wishes during the few days he is in this world. The residents of Kufa were well aware that Mu'awiyah's son had neither associated with good men or pious Muslims nor been provided with the appropriate family upbringing required for a leader. Yazid was so renowned for his wrongdoing and unwise character throughout the Islamic society that when Mu'awiyah intended to force the elite of the Muslim community, threatening them by sword, to make a pledge of allegiance with Yazid, he gave a praising description of his son, and then Imam Hussain, who was among the crowd, said:

> *O Mu'awiyah! Say things about Yazid that are true about him and his character. You are trying to hide something that the sun has cast light upon; these things are as clear as day. That is enough! The end of your life is near, so leave people alone and let them think of how to lead their own lives.*

When a group of Shiite men gathered at Sulaiman ibn Surad's house, Sulaiman told them, "You are Shiites who follow Hussain and also his father. Write to him and invite him here only if you truly mean to help him; otherwise, do not deceive him."

What made Sulaiman make such a serious suggestion was the long reputation the people of Kufa had in shameful disputes, pitiful disagreements, and also how they had changed and purged their own words regarding

---

[187] Muhaddith Qumi, *Nafas ul-Mahmum*, quoted from Shaikh Mufid. Also see Ibn Al-Athir's *Al-Kamil fil-Tarikh*, Vol. 2.

There is some dispute over the number of letters sent by the people of Kufa to invite Imam Hussain (PBUH) to join them. Some narrators have reported there to have been over 2,000 letters.

[188] Muhaddith Qumi, *Nafas ul-Mahmum*, quoted from Shaikh Mufid. Also see Ibn Al-Athir's *Al-Kamil fil-Tarikh*, Vol. 2.

Imam Ali (PBUH) and his son Imam Hassan Mujtaba (PBUH).

As a matter of fact, Sulaiman's prediction came true, and the people of Kufa – except for a very few – proved unfaithful regarding the letters they had written and the pledges they had made. They confronted the Holy Prophet's offspring, fought him in the most wicked and terrible way that is only imaginable for animals, and martyred him most appallingly.

In Sermon 25 of the *Nahjulbalaghah*, Imam Ali (PBUH) has severely scolded the people of Kufa for their inactive attitude toward gravely bitter incidents, and in Sermons 48 and 101, he describes Kufa as the city where major, stormy, and erupting events take place. However, in other cases in which Imam Ali has praised his pure, diligent men, several of them were from Kufa. Even in the bloody event of Karbala, some of the finest men of Kufa were fighting alongside Imam Hussain (PBUH).

A Brief Study of the Residents of Kufa at That Time

The people of a society can obviously not be identified and described by means of a certain set of fixed characteristics, for people have the potential to be flexible, and external factors also bring about change in them. Therefore, an absolute set of theorems about the people of a society cannot be achieved. Of course, the more the machine-like aspects there are in the lives of the people of society, their potential for flexibility and the influence of various external factors will also decrease, and it will, therefore, be easier for those in charge of such societies to identify and describe their people. On the other hand, the more strongly is human beings' lives based on their individual identity and their diverse choices and decisions, the greater their flexibility and change will be in regard to factors bringing about change, unless the principles, laws, values, and virtues managing the people of a society have infiltrated within them and justify their actions. The obligation to observe principles, rules, and values is one of the reasons why the human beings of a society achieve development, evolution, and growth.

Thus, intelligible order and reasonable discipline in life are based upon one of the two following factors:

1. When the machine-like aspects and dimensions of the lives of the people in a society begin to work, the potential for flexibility and the ability to be influenced by factors of change are disrupted and disabled. Such a lifestyle, which can nowadays be seen in the West and some cases in the East, arises as the result of several factors. This form of life has the advantage of making order and discipline a reality in people's life, which is highly fruitful and important. The flaw of this lifestyle, on the other hand, is that it disables individuals' true essence and personal identity, which thus leads to the disruption of free will. In other words, people drown in a kind of order and discipline which in fact neutralizes their main identity and their personal essence; they live a fatalistic or semi-fatalistic life.
2. If the people achieve such a high level of spiritual perfection and

mental development – by means of receiving training and education on values and virtues – they shall understand, through their innate reason, ration, and conscience, that it is immensely essential to lead a life of order and discipline.

Now let us focus on the social life of the people of Kufa during that era. As mentioned above, it is impossible to identify and describe the people of a society in general and throughout all of history by means of certain, absolute characteristics, even if we attempt to do so with extensive statistics. It seems that the people of Kufa at that time were, as were some people in other Islamic communities, lacking in the order and discipline which allows the future characteristics of society be identified and described to a suitable extent. Imam Ali (PBUH) was by no means someone who would disable the personal identity of the people and use despotic domination in order to rule over them as helpless cogs of a machine. On the other hand, not all of those people were mature and developed enough mentally to be able to use their conscience, common sense and reason, as well as Imam Ali's teachings – which followed the same style as the Holy Prophet (PBUH), did – in order to use Islam's principles and values in their lives. After Imam Ali's reign, the rulers appointed by the Umayyads, who lacked both religious and political piety, were incapable of activating the reason and conscience of the residents of Kufa as well as other Islamic communities in order to make intelligible life a reality and have the public live a life of discipline and order. On the other hand, they were not able to eradicate the basic roots of the fundamental rules of life in all people, either. As a result, weak characters on one hand and faith in the finest principles of life and its values and virtues, on the other hand, were a natural phenomenon among the people of Kufa at that time.

Now we understand the value of Sulaiman ibn Surad's words to the people of Kufa who had gathered at the door of his house:

> Give it some thought. If you are absolutely certain that you will help Imam Hussain and defend his supreme goal, write to him and ask that he come here. However, if you think that you will not be able to fulfill the duty you are undertaking regarding him, do not invite him here.[189]

Imam Hussain (PBUH) Asked Allah for Help on His Journey to Iraq

When the letters of invitation to Iraq were complete, Imam Hussain prayed to Allah, asking the Lord for help on the crucial journey he had coming up.[190]

---

[189] Ibid.

[190] Ibid. When Abdullah ibn Muti' asked Imam Hussain (PBUH) where he would be heading for, Imam Hussain (PBUH) replied, "For now, I am heading toward Macca, and then I shall ask Allah to show me the best path." It seems this was why Imam Hussain (PBUH) prayed to Allah here.

Therefore, Imam Hussain's request for the best fate possible from Allah was, in fact, the direct intuitive perception of what was the best path for him, which Imam Hussain (PBUH) had no doubt was heading toward Iraq. Likewise, the Holy Prophet Abraham (PBUH) asked Allah to provide him with intuition and total serenity in his heart by allowing him to directly see how Allah brought the dead back to life on Judgment Day. The following verse of the Holy Quran points out what Abraham said:

> *"Show me, Lord, how You will raise the dead." Allah replied, "Have you no faith?" He said, "Yes, but just to reassure my heart."*[191]

Imam Hussain (PBUH) then wrote the following letter and had Hani ibn Hani and Sa'id ibn Abdullah, the last dispatches from the people of Kufa, deliver it to them:

> *In the Name of Allah, the Compassionate, the Merciful.*
> *This is a letter from Hussain, the son of Ali, to all Muslims and all of the faithful. Praise and gratitude to Allah, and peace be upon the Holy Prophet. Hani and Sa'id, the last deliverers of your letters, arrived, and I am aware of everything you have pointed out in the letters. All of you stated that you had no Imam, no leader. You asked me to come to your city, so that I may be the means for Allah to bless you with His guidance toward righteousness. I am sending my brother, my cousin, Muslim ibn Aqil, a trustee of mine, who is also a member of my family, to you. I have ordered him to write to me about your views, opinions and the state you are in. If he informs me that the point of view of the majority of the public and the wisest and most reasonable of you conforms with what the letters I have received indicate, I shall soon join you. I swear on my life that a divine leader is one who judges and decides based on the holy book sent by Allah, upholds justice, is devoted and dedicated to Allah's righteous religion, and uses his own soul as a witness to his oaths.*[192]

Imam Hussain's letter has been addressed to the residents of Kufa and all Muslims and faithful people. This shows that it was not only the Shiites but in fact the whole Muslim community who requested that Imam Hussain (PBUH) move to Kufa. The vast popularity Imam Hussain (PBUH) had across all Islamic societies – which we have already shown – is proof for such a demand. Moreover, the number of the letters, signatures, and the importance of the figures who had written or signed them was so great that, regardless of other factors and incentives, they provided grounds logical enough to necessitate a move to Kufa and begin an uprising involving the people there.

---

[191] The Cow (2:260)
[192] Muhaddith Qumi, *Nafas ul-Mahmum*, quoted from Shaikh Mufid. Also see Ibn Al-Athir's *Al-Kamil fil-Tarikh*, Vol. 2.

Indeed, only the sacred life which depends upon Allah is worth swearing by.

There is no doubt that, in all countries and all peoples, people swear on things regarded as sacred, for such oaths prove something to be true. We hear such phrases frequently every day – "I swear on my life, on my father's life, on my mother's life, on my child's life" – but if we consider them carefully, it is the importance and preciousness of life that is of significance to the one taking the oath rather than its sacred nature. As we know, the importance and necessity of truth are separate from its greatness, sacredness or dignity.

Having examined the history of Imam Hussain's life and his relationship with Allah, all historians, authorities on the analysis of history and thinkers studying great figures of history have recognized his character as one worthy of swearing by, because:

Anyone who – no matter what situation or state their body may be in – is in prostration in spirit is worth swearing by.

Part 22

The Conditions Needed for One to Become the Divine Leader of Allah's Subjects

I swear on my life that only he who rules and decrees based on the Holy Book can be a divine leader.

As seen by the political philosophy of human beings' natural life and the normal flow of history, such a statement will conflict with the approach taken by the philosophy of managing the "intelligible life" of human beings as Allah's creations.

In order to better understand the differences between these two points of view, we must first realize the difference between pioneer culture and dependent culture in life. In other words, we must admit that:

1. Since dependent culture is based on people's purely natural desires people and the limited knowledge they achieve throughout history, it involves no obligations or guidelines to help a man achieve the perfection the seeds for which have already been instilled within human beings.

Such a way of life does not take dignity, honor, the expansion and development of the human character regarding the universe, dependence upon Allah, the divine sense of obligation toward keeping promises and following one's pure conscience, affection for one's fellow human beings, or any other values or virtues into consideration except as far as what is appropriate to serve the management of purely natural life – where the material aspect is focused on "gaining as much physical and material pleasure as possible" and the mental aspect believes that "I am the end and others are the means".

To rule in such a society, in which the culture described above prevails, there is no doubt that the only prerequisite is the ability to provide people with such a way of life. It must be noted, of course, that this kind of management will be able to work provided that the ruler does not intend to indulge in the absolute fulfillment of his own desires; in other words, he must not have been trained according to the thoughts of men like Thomas Hobbes, Nero, Genghis Khan, Tamerlane, or Caligula. Otherwise, people's lives will be based on the dependent culture of leviathans[193] – that is, if such a

---

[193] The largest, strongest animal imaginable, one that can dominate other animals and sacrifice them to the advantage of its own desirable life.

way of living can be called life! To provide an example, can there be a clearer one than Yazid's rule, in which people were compelled to be his slaves?

2. Life-based on intelligible, pioneer culture. If a society is endowed with this form of life – which is dependent upon rays of divine perfection – it is impossible to lead unless the divine aspect is taken into consideration. The leader may not even be infallible like holy prophets and Imams; nonetheless, the significance and necessity of their governance have been noted since the earliest of times, and the finest of human virtues and traits have been regarded as essential for those who intend to rule. Men like Plato, for instance, knew this very well. Imam Ali's order to Malik Ashtar regarding his mission to serve as the governor of Egypt is a fine example of the conditions and qualities a leader must have.[194]

In his letter to the people of Kufa, Imam Hussain (PBUH) has pointed out four basic conditions to be met:

1. judging and ruling based on Allah's book,
2. upholding justice,
3. religious faith, and
4. dependence of the soul upon Allah.

1. Judging and Ruling Based on Allah's Book

This is the last holy book Allah has sent people through the Prophet of Islam. This is the book which clearly depicts a man in view of the four relationships (man's relationship with Allah, with the universe, with his own self and with other human beings) both in the realm of clarifying "what there is" and in the realm of "what there should be." It is obvious that only through such a significant knowledge will man be able to find answers to the six basic questions: 1. Who am I? 2. Where have I come from? 3. Why have I come here? 4. Where have I come to? 5. Who am I with? 6. Where do I go from here?

It should never be stated that a large majority of people live their lives without having found the answers to the questions mentioned above or even having felt the need to understand these questions or the four relationships, for one who says such things do not seem to see any difference between the cogs of an unconscious machine and a human being endowed with knowledge, freedom and a sense of duty! It is quite obvious, of course, that when man is deprived of character and human identity and is thus forced

---

[194] There is a highly significant point which must be noted here. People's lives must be based upon intelligible culture rather than dependent culture; nonetheless, this does not mean that people are not entitled to determine the quality of their desired lives. In other words, this idea does not diminish intelligible democracy. In fact, it endeavors to enhance people's characters to such a level that of ideals and knowledge that they can distinguish – in line with intelligible life – what is appropriate for their lives from what is not and live based on such principles.

to live in a machine-like aspect [in other words, when man is compelled to live a machine-like life], not only will such a being fail to understand the four relationships or the six questions, but he will even find it impossible to comprehend whether he exists or not! Nevertheless, man exists, as do the laws that have brought about human beings and manage them. Whether man likes it or not, the law of the purposeful universe – which states that every human being, with no exceptions, shall one day stand responsible for his actions – applies to man. Now how could Yazid fall in line with Allah's book?!

2. Upholding Justice

> *Whoever is unjust is, in fact, a wolf rather than human;*
> *In such a case, we must hope for justice from Allah, for there is none*
> *of that in the world ...*

The Holy Quran reads:

> **The word of thy Lord doth find its fulfillment in truth and justice; nothing can change His words.**[195]

Intelligible, objective being is based upon justice. It is justice that allows all of the man's constructive potentials and talents, whether in his individual or social life, to flourish. Moreover, the main essence of the order prevailing over the universe is also justice.

Having been endowed and blessed with the chance to exist, which is Allah's immense blessing to mankind, there is nothing else as essential as justice for the descendants of Adam. Throughout all of history, whenever there has been development or flourish, it has occurred as a result of justice. On the other hand, whenever mankind has suffered from decadence, retardation, or demise, the bloody claws of oppression can be seen choking advocates of justice. Therefore, from now onward, let us now add another form of categorization to the categorizations existing regarding the rises or falls human societies have experienced. This new approach to categorization involves eras of the flourish of justice, including its various kinds, or the lack of flourish of justice in society. This kind of categorization may provide us with a solution so that we may finally understand why civilizations in the twenty-first century rise or fall.

In the Holy Quran, it has been pointed out on numerous occasions that the demise of civilizations and the destruction of peoples and societies who flourished on the earth for long or short periods of time is the result of their wrongdoing:

> **Generations before you, we destroyed when they did wrong.**[196]

---

[195] Cattle (6:115).
[196] Jonah (10:13).

Did Yazid understand that justice provides the pillars for objective being?! Did it ever occur to his mind that it is justice which allows all constructive human potentials, whether in individual or social life, flourish and become a reality? Could he fathom that justice is the main essence of the order prevailing over the universe? Was Yazid brought up in a way that he could learn to merely realize that there was a world besides his own "purely natural self," let alone understand that such a world was based on justice?!

Do those – like the judge Abu Bakr ibn Al-Arabi[197] – who attempt to show Yazid as innocent and display him as a ruler whom all Islamic societies were supposed to obey not realize that they, in fact, share Yazid's crime by doing so? The only difference is that Yazid murdered and mutilated the bodies of Imam Hussain (PBUH) and 72 of his men, while people like the judge ibn Al-Arabi are murdering and mutilating human values, a crime which will lead to the annihilation of the souls of millions of human beings! Have you ever pondered that such use of science and knowledge in order to decree that no one should damn or condemn Yazid (something Ghazali unfortunately did) is, in fact, the worst possible way to abuse science and knowledge in order to approve one of the most shameful, wicked faces in history? Some say that Yazid may have repented! People like Ghazali should be asked, "Can one secretly repent for a crime that has led to the misleading of millions of human beings?" Is the punishment for deliberate murder not eternal pain and suffering in hell? Obviously, if one is to suffer eternal pain in hell, one is prone to damnation and condemning as well. Apparently, a man like Ghazali, with the information and knowledge he had, must have had another purpose by preventing people from damning and condemning Yazid. Perhaps he meant to stop people from insulting those who brought Yazid to power, such as Mu'awiyah.

3. Religious Faith

Allah's righteous religion is the general, divine religion which was

---

[197] Abu Bakr ibn al-Arabi, (born in Sevilla in 1076 and died in Fez in 1148) was a judge and scholar of Maliki law from al-Andalus. In his book Al-'Awasim min al-Qawasim ("Defense Against Disaster"), as quoted by Ibn Khaldun, he has written: "If only Hussain, the son of Ali, the greatest man among these people and the son of the greatest man of this land, had stayed at home or taken up farming or raising animals. Even if the public or Ibn Abbas and Abdullah ibn Umar had asked him to begin a campaign to uphold righteousness, he should have refused, and instead, he should have heeded the words of the Holy Prophet (who had warned about the arising of such conspiracies). If only he had remembered how the Holy Prophet had praised Hassan ibn Ali's truce; if only he had considered the fact that even Hassan ibn Ali had failed to keep the caliphate and the government despite all of the troops he had. Now how could Hussain have taken over the caliphate with the help of the wrongdoers and hooligans of Kufa? (If he had considered these points, such an unfortunate, pitiful event would never have occurred.)"

revealed upon great prophets of Allah such as Adam, Noah, Moses, Jesus and Muhammad, the son of Abdullah, may peace be upon them, in order to provide the grounds for man's happiness and prosperity both in this world and in the afterworld. Allah's righteous religion is not the deceiving facades and slogans which have proven to be the greatest factor leading man toward misery, disabling the most valuable asset human beings have – the ability to be absorbed by Allah's divine attraction. It does not involve the empty, futile theorems and propositions presented in order to deprive people of their material, physical and spiritual rights. Nor does Allah's righteous religion include the sorceries and forms of magic which, due to their irreconcilable contradictions with knowledge and science, have also brought about the demise of men of science and knowledge.

4. The Dependence of the Soul upon Allah

This divine relationship is the truth pointed out in the following verse of the Holy Quran:

> *Truly, my prayer and my service of sacrifice, my life, and my death, are [all] for Allah, the Cherisher of the Worlds.*[198]

To realize how important this condition is, we must first understand, through internal thought and soul-searching, that we all, as stated in the Holy Quran, *"come from Allah and eventually return to Allah,"* and that this is the only interpretation possible for human life and death in the universe. It can be stated, without any prejudice toward any religion, that no school of thought or thinker in any human society has been able to come up with such a formula to justify, interpret and point out the ultimate aim of the life and death of human beings. This verse means that we humans are beings whose life and death depends upon Allah's wisdom, will and blessing – thus, it is not just limited to our "coming from Allah and returning to Allah" and nothing else.[199] The management of such an immense, divine process should be undertaken by those whose egos, characters, souls, and lives depend upon Allah. There is no doubt that Hussain (PBUH) was a man worthy of such a position, and not Yazid, whom credible accounts of history have described as being dependent upon his dogs, monkeys, musical instruments, frivolities, and the excitement of his animal instincts.

It was probably around this time that Imam Hussain's letter to the people

---

[198] Cattle (6:162).

[199] This is the nihilistic point of view that has remained from ancient Greece. Even some poetry attributed to Khayyam depicts this approach toward life:

> *After some time, we changed from a child to a master,*
>
> *and we reveled in our mastery for a while.*
>
> *Now hear about the end of the story and what finally came upon us:*
>
> *we came from the soil and we went back into the soil …*

of Basra was sent. In any case, Sayyid ibn Tawus has reported that:

> *Imam Hussain (PBUH) wrote a letter to a group of the elite in Basra*
> *and had Sulaiman, whose agnomen was Abu Razin, deliver it. In*
> *the letter, Imam Hussain had invited the elite of Basra, including*
> *Yazid ibn Masud Nahshali and Munzir ibn Jarud Abdi, to help and*
> *follow him. Yazid ibn Masud summoned the Bani Tamim, the Bani*
> *Hanzalah and the Bani Sa'd. He asked the Bani Tamim what they*
> *thought of him. The Bani Tamim responded that they regarded him*
> *as a man of great dignity and honor. "I have called you here," Yazid*
> *ibn Masud then said, "regarding a highly significant matter on*
> *which I need your consultation and your help."*
> *"We swear to Allah," they replied, "that we only want the best for*
> *you, and we shall go out of our way to give you the best opinions*
> *possible. Now tell us, and we will listen."*
> *"Mu'awiyah has died," Yazid ibn Masud said, "and I swear to Allah*
> *that he died a lowly, lost man. Beware that with him dead, violations*
> *and sins have been broken down, and the pillars of oppression have*
> *been shaken up. He created a pledge of allegiance [for his son Yazid],*
> *and I believe he assumed [in his own mind at least] that it was firmly*
> *established. May Allah forbid such a pledge of allegiance becoming a*
> *reality. His efforts will fail, and the consultations he has made in this*
> *regard will also lead to nothing but disgrace and vain. Mu'awiyah's*
> *son, Yazid, the wine-drinking leader of the corrupt, has risen to claim*
> *himself to be the ruler of the Muslims, without even having their*
> *own consent! Considering his qualities, Yazid is an unworthy man,*
> *a man voids of any knowledge. He is a man who will never decide*
> *righteously; he is totally incapable of telling right from wrong. I*
> *swear to Allah that it is a fact that campaigning to overthrow him*
> *is even better than fighting against unbelievers. Hussain, the son*
> *of Ali and the Prophet's daughter, on the other hand, is a man of*
> *fine, original upbringing and a man of knowledge. Indeed, he is the*
> *most deserving man to rule, for he has a long and fine reputation*
> *for advocating and advancing Islam, and when it comes to the Holy*
> *Prophet, no man existing now can claim to be as close to the Prophet*
> *than he was. He is kind to everyone, whether they are children or the*
> *elderly. He deserves to guide and be the Imam of the society, and it*
> *is through him that Allah shall see us as worthy of heaven, and shall*
> *advise us through him. Therefore, do not fall astray from the light*
> *of righteousness and the path of Allah; do not allow yourself to be*
> *engulfed in the hardships and troubles of wrongdoing. If Sakhr ibn*
> *Qais caused you disgrace in the Jamal incident, come and help the*
> *Prophet's offspring, may that clear away your previous disgrace. I*
> *swear to Allah that whoever does not help Hussain shall see himself*
> *disgraced by Allah and his offspring reduced. I shall now prepare for*

battle. I will don my armor and ready myself to help Hussain. Beware that those who do not get killed shall die one day, and those who flee cannot flee death. May Allah bless you. Give me an appropriate reply."

The Bani Hanzalah, Bani Tamim and Bani Sa'd's response to Yazid ibn Masud was quite positive. They were in total agreement with his suggestion. Yazid ibn Masud then wrote a letter to Imam Hussain (PBUH):

Praise be to Allah, and may peace be upon the Prophet. I received your letter, and now I understood what you asked me to do – to be endowed and blessed by obeying you, and achieve emancipation by helping you. It is certain that Allah will never allow the earth to be empty of true endeavours of the path of perfection and goodness and guides to the path of deliverance for mankind. Indeed, you are Allah's signs, His blessings upon the earth. Muhammad is like a tree, and you are the branches of that olive tree. Muhammad is the roots, and you are the branches. Now ride the wings of the angel of happiness and prosperity and come over to our land. I have the necks of the Bani Tamim bent down ready to obey you. Their enthusiasm to follow you is even greater than the willingness of thirsty camels to reach water. I have also had the Bani Sa'd agree to submit to your command. The contamination in their hearts have been washed away with the downpour of your blessing.

"What a spiritual rejoicing you have been overcome by!" Imam Hussain (PBUH) remarked when reading Yazid ibn Masud's letter. "May Allah keep you safe and dear on Judgment Day. May you be fulfilled on the Day of the Great Thirst."

Yazid ibn Masud prepared to go and help Imam Hussain (PBUH). Before he reached his destination, however, he heard that Imam Hussain (PBUH) had been martyred. Yazid ibn Masud began crying out in despair and sorrow.[200]

The sincere, pure, meaningful letter Yazid ibn Masud Nahshali wrote to Imam Hussain (PBUH) is one of the finest and clearest examples proving why Imam Hussain (PBUH) was the greatest and the most deserving man to rule the Islamic communities. It also depicts, quite vividly and firmly and from a variety of aspects, how undeserving Yazid ibn Mu'awiyah was to rule. Let us consider the following sentences once again:

It is certain that Allah will never allow the earth to be empty of true endeavours of the path of perfection and goodness and guides to the path of deliverance for mankind. Indeed, you are Allah's signs, His blessings upon the earth. Muhammad is like a tree, and you are the branches of that olive tree. Muhammad is the roots, and you are the

[200] Muhaddith Qumi, *Nafas ul-Mahmum.*

*branches. Now ride the wings of the angel of happiness and prosperity
and come over to our land.*

Imam Hussain summoned Muslim ibn Aqil and had him, Qays ibn Musahir
Al Saidawi, and a few other men set out for Kufa. He ordered them to
be pious and righteous, be kind to the people and prevents anyone from
finding out what the true purpose of the mission was. Muslim ibn Aqil came
to Madina, said prayers in the Prophet's Mosque, bid his family farewell and
hired two guides from Qais's tribe. The two guides lost the way, however,
and they were too thirsty to go on. They showed Muslim which way he had
to go. Muslim kept on going, and the two guides died of dehydration. In a
place known as Maziq, Muslim wrote Imam Hussain (PBUH) a letter and
had Qays ibn Musahir Al Saidawi deliver it. The letter read:

> *Praise be to Allah, and may peace be upon the Prophet. I left Madina
> accompanied by two guides. The two guides lost the way, and we
> were very thirsty. Soon, the guides died. We kept going, but we barely
> saved ourselves. We found water in a place called Maziq, which is
> located in the oasis known as Khabt. I found this incident as a bad
> omen. Kindly allow me to be relieved from this mission, and have
> someone else do it instead. May peace be upon you.*

When Imam Hussain (PBUH) received the letter, he wrote back to Muslim:

> *Praise be to Allah, and may peace be upon the Prophet. I fear that
> the reason why you were made to resign from the mission I gave you
> and write to me was that you are afraid. Keep on going. May peace
> be with you.*

Muslim read Imam Hussain's reply and thought, "If fear made me feel
a bad omen, I am not afraid." He kept on going. He reached a source of
water which belonged to the Tay tribe, and after a brief stopover, he was
on his way again. Soon he saw a man shoot an arrow at deer. The deer
fell to the ground. "Allah-willing," Muslim thought, "we shall defeat our
enemy as well." When he arrived in Kufa, it was the fifth day of the month of
Shawwal.[201] [Muslim had left Madina halfway into the month of Ramadan.]
He stayed in the house of Mukhtar ibn Abi Ubaydah. Shiites frequented
there to see him. When a group of Shiites gathered before Muslim, he read
Imam Hussain's letter to them, which brought them to tears.[202]

Regarding Muslim ibn Aqil's character and his worthiness for this
mission, it is enough just to consider how Imam Hussain (PBUH) introduces
him. In his letter to the people of Kufa, Imam Hussain writes, "I am sending
my brother, my cousin, and the most trusted man in my clan, Muslim ibn
Aqil, to you."

---

[201] As reported by Masudi in his *Muruj-ul Thahab*.
[202] As reported in Muhaddith Qumi's *Nafas ul-Mahmum* and Ibn Al-Athir's *Al-Kamil fil Tarikh*, Vol. 4.

There are highly important concepts hidden in Imam Hussain's calling Muslim "my brother" and "the most trusted man." In short, every word Muslim said, everything he did and every aspect of his behavior during this mission was to be regarded as Imam Hussain's. On the other hand, his sense of duty and the extreme hardships he went through in order to accomplish his mission clearly prove the strength of his character and how deserving he was to serve as Imam Hussain's delegate.

The other significant point which needs to be considered is that Imam Hussain's deserving delegate, this great man who had been quite appropriately appointed to represent the leader of the martyrs of humanity, was martyred in the most horrific and appallingly possible way during the stormy events of Kufa without ever giving into them. Muslim never expressed any regret or discomfort about the bloody events of Kufa; nor did he ever claim that he had been forced to come to Kufa. Therefore, Muslim's taking the death of his two guides due to dehydration and thirst as a bad omen as well as his considering the hunting of the deer as a good sign can be regarded as passing mental phenomena, which is quite normal for non-infallible in times of dire straits. Despite the many advantages this great man had – which had made him become the most deserving man to represent Imam Hussain (PBUH), the divine leader of his time – Muslim lacked the divine feeling Imam Hussain (PBUH) had, the feeling which arises out of the knowledge Imams are endowed with and makes life and death seem like two kinds of happiness and prosperity ("one of the two good choices"). This is why he never went through any imaginations, illusions or hallucinations which could contradict such a feeling. Considering the response Imam Hussain (PBUH) wrote for Muslim ibn Aqil – ordering him to avoid fear and keep on with his mission – and the serenity Muslim found having received Imam Hussain's answer, we understand that Muslim had undertaken and begun his mission with total faith in Imam Hussain (PBUH) and his command, and later faced martyrdom in the most terrible way and through the most horrific crimes.

Many people came to see Muslim, and there were frequent gatherings. Whenever a new group of people arrived, Muslim would read them Imam Hussain's letter, which would bring them to tears and make them promise to help Imam Hussain (PBUH) battle his enemies. Then Abis ibn Abi Shabib Shakiri, may whom Allah bless, rose up and said:

> Praise be to Allah. I cannot say anything on people's behalf, for I do not know what goes on in their hearts and minds, and I have no intention of deceiving you through them. I swear to Allah that I am informing you of what I have prepared my own soul for. I swear to Allah that I shall join you if you ask me to. I shall help you, fight your enemies, and use my sword until I meet Almighty Allah. The only reward I want is to get close to Allah.[203]

---

[203] Muhaddith Qumi, *Nafas ul-Mahmum.*

Why can those who are fascinated by true anthropological knowledge, those infatuated with progressing the pioneer culture of evolution, not disturb the peace and quiet of those books resting on the bookshelves for a few minutes? Why don't we stop drowning in appealing jargon – which in fact effectively intensify the existing ambiguities – and focus on the realities about human beings instead? We should put aside all sophistries and double talk and move toward righteousness and truth. Let us recognize the immensity of the human virtue which can provide man with such independent identity and character than he will not feel the need for anyone to accompany him along the path to becoming a true "human being."

Such a character can be regarded as the soul of souls; the one literature has been searching for in order to present the role model for the true pilgrim of righteousness and truth. Abis ibn Abi Shabib Shakiri was such a man. As an educated reader, you have certainly read many things about the significance of human existence in the universe as well as the amazing potentials and faculties this known – and from many aspects unknown – being has. Writing these words, I assume that you are a sincere seeker of original truths about mankind, the manifestation of the divine will; therefore, I would be obliged if you would take the words of this great man into more careful consideration:

> I cannot say anything on people's behalf, for I do not know what goes on in their hearts and minds, and I have no intention of deceiving you through them. I swear to Allah that I am informing you of what I have prepared my own soul for… the only reward I want is to get close to Allah.

In other words, Abis is saying that he does not need people's conformation, assistance or collaboration in order to achieve the truth for which he lives for. His life has been given to him by Allah, not due to the permission or the cooperation of the people. Human beings are dependent upon their natural fellow beings only until they are attracted by Allah's divine rays. From then on, human beings associate and interact with emancipated souls and angels – those deserving to enter such a field of attraction. This is the same fundamental principle stating that human beings derive the greatest power of all from inside their own selves, thus making them needless of any other power.

"May Allah bless you," Habib ibn Mazahir told Abis. "You stated your intentions in brief words." Then he turned toward the people and said, "I swear to the One Allah that I have the same opinion as Abis does," and the others agreed as well… 18,000 people in Kufa pledged allegiance with Muslim ibn Aqil. Muslim wrote to Imam Hussain (PBUH), informing him about the people's pledge of allegiance and suggesting that the Imam should leave for Kufa. From the time people made their pledge of allegiance and the sending of this letter until Muslim's martyrdom, 27 days had passed. As the people taking sides with him amassed in number, the place Muslim was staying was no longer a secret due to the frequent visits people made there."[204]

It is obvious that had things gone on like that, Kufa would have – as the Bani Umayyad had felt it would – totally freed itself from the control of Damascus; in fact, all of Iraq would have confronted Damascus. Imam Hussain (PBUH) was extremely popular among the public, and on the other hand, Yazid's character was flawed spiritually and culturally. Moreover, the two following points should also be taken into consideration:

1. Ali, the son of Abi Talib, was a man of immense character and the true leader of Islamic societies;

2. The Umayyads, and Mu'awiyyah first and foremost, presented the religion of Islam as well as its moral and cultural aspects in a limited way to advance and strengthen their own government rather than out of obligation. Therefore, a kind of active conflict and contrast had arisen between the Umayyads and the deep levels of the society. It was thus natural for intense preventive measures to be taken if a revolution were to stir up in Kufa, or any other city.

Nu'man ibn Bashir, who had been appointed by Mu'awiyyah as the governor of Kufa and Yazid had approved that he keeps on serving in that position, delivered a sermon to the people. Having given praise to Allah, he said, "O servants of Allah! Be pious, and do not rush to cause riots and rancor, for it is rioting and disruption which leads to loss of life, bloodshed and the usurpation of property. I shall not fight anyone who does not intend to fight me and shall cause no discomfort for anyone who intends to cause me no discomfort. I will not disturb those who are asleep; I will not attack you, and I will not persecute anyone by suspicion or allegation. However, if you were to confront me, break your pledge of allegiance, and oppose your leader, I swear to the One Allah that I shall strike down upon you as long as there is a sword in my hand, even if I have to do so alone. I hope that the number of you who know what is righteous is higher than those who shall be killed by wrongdoers."

It is quite astonishing how Nu'man ibn Bashir uses two incredibly significant virtues in order to force Allah's servants to obey Yazid:

1. He advises them to "be pious." What kind of piety is this?! Do obey a corrupt, morally deviated man who opposes Islam and falling astray from righteousness, dignity, honor, and divine justice mean being pious?! He tells people not protest, be calm, and allow the government to do as it pleases! Instead of such statements, other statements can be used in order to convey what they truly mean – Whatever despotic tyrants wish is righteous! Every move made by people and their very lives are at the service of the desires of the ruler! Those who confront tyrannical despots shall meet their death!

If people were to see their rights fulfilled and observed by tyrants and oppressors throughout history quite easily and comfortably and without

---

[204] Ibid.

having to go through sincere efforts and genuine sacrifices, would it be possible for anyone other than men of power and their mercenaries to live throughout history? Would it be possible for even the slightest of strides to be taken in order to develop and enhance the lives of human beings?!

2. The other word Nu'man ibn Bashir uses quite cunningly is the "righteousness." This sacred word has been abused since the earliest of times, particularly when it comes to politics. One of the most wicked features about wrongdoers in the history of humanity has been how they have abused the sacred word "righteousness" in order to trample people's true rights.

Abdullah ibn Muslim ibn Rabi'ah, an ally of the Umayyads, rose up and said, "What you need to do calls for a firm decision. Such an approach toward one's enemies is the way the incompetent behave."

Nu'man replied, however, "I would rather be incompetent in obeying Allah than being competent in sins," and stepped down from his elevated sermon position. Abdullah ibn Muslim wrote to Yazid ibn Mu'awiyah, informing him that Muslim ibn Aqil had arrived in Kufa and that Hussain's Shiite followers had made a pledge of allegiance with him. "If you need Kufa," he wrote, "send someone powerful to Kufa to carry out your orders, for Nu'man ibn Bashir is either an incompetent man or pretending to be incompetent." Ammara ibn Aqabah and Umar ibn Sa'd wrote similar letters to Yazid as well. Having received the letters, Yazid summoned Serjun – who had served Mu'awiyah – and said, "Hussain has sent Muslim ibn Aqil to Kufa. What do you think? I have also received word that Nu'man ibn Bashir is a weak man, or maybe he is pretending to be weak. He had made some inappropriate remarks as well.[205]"

"If I show you a treaty left from Mu'awiyah," Serjun said, "will you execute it?"

"Yes, I will," Yazid replied.

Serjun showed him a letter in which Mu'awiyah had appointed Ibn Ziyad as the governor of Kufa. "Mu'awiyah died, but he had ordered that Ibn Ziyad become the governor of two cities (Basra and Kufa)."

"I shall do the same then," Yazid said. "Send the order to Ibn Ziyad." Yazid then attached a letter of his own to Mu'awiyah's directive as well. The letter read, "My followers residing in Kufa have written to me, stating that Aqil's son is busy gathering people around himself as an effort to create a schism among Muslims. Receiving this letter, you are to leave for Kufa, apprehend Aqil's son, and either restrain him, kill him or send him away on exile."

Muslim ibn Amr headed toward Basra and delivered the order and the

---

[205] What Yazid meant here by Nu'man's inappropriate remarks may have been his last statement in his sermon, "I would rather be incompetent in obeying Allah than be competent in sins." On the other hand, it may have been another remark he made, which has been reported by Ibn Qutaybah Dinwari in his work *Al-Imamah wa' Al-Siyasah*, Vol. 2 – "The son of the Prophet's daughter is more popular to us than Bajdal's son." Maysun bint Bajdal al-Kulaibi was Yazid's mother's name.

letter to Ubaidullah. Ubaidullah immediately prepared to leave for Kufa. The next day, having severely threatened the people of Basra about any wrongdoing in his absence[206], he headed toward Kufa.[207]

Nu'man ibn Bashir's statement – "I would rather be incompetent in obeying Allah than being competent in sins" – can be restated, with a more accurate interpretation, as the valuable strength within those who avoid taking any actions or making any decisions despite the sense of obligation they feel due to Allah's orders. On the other hand, those who act and decide based on their selfish lusts and their submission to their "natural self" and animal desires are weak, even though they may be regarded as powerful when it comes to affluence and financial resources. Therefore, we must say that the most powerful are those who can control and possess their own selves, even though they may have no possessions in this world at all. One may own the whole world, however, and fail to possess one's own self; such a person should be considered as the weakest of all. Unfortunately, the history of man's conduct shows that human beings have always shamefully preferred the possession of external objects – no matter how qualitatively or quantitatively meager they may have been – to the possession of their own selves. Have you ever noticed that all oppressions and murders throughout history have arisen out of the disruption of external possessions? Had man's control and possession of his own self-fallen in line with general education and serious development, human beings would undoubtedly not only see the power injustice and regard powerful people as just and fair ones, but they would also justify the progression of history as a path toward evolution.

Thus, we must say that Nu'man ibn Bashir, considering the words quoted from him here, was a powerful man who pretended to be weak.

If the letter Serjun showed Yazid had been truly written by Mu'awiyah, it could be regarded as definitive, concrete evidence that Mu'awiyah had reckoned that the day would come when Kufa would embrace Imam Hussain's rule against his son Yazid and that the Umayyads would be at the peril of being overthrown. Therefore, he had decided to appoint the bloodthirsty Ubaidullah Ibn Ziyad, a man renowned for his ruthless animosity toward the good men in the Islamic society and his support from the Umayyad clan, as an effort to eradicate such an uprising.

Accompanied by 500 men from Basra, including Abdullah ibn Al-Harith ibn Nowafil and Sharik ibn Al-A'war who were Shiite followers of Imam Ali (PBUH), Ubaidullah Ibn Ziyad headed for Kufa. Muslim ibn Amr Al-Bahili and his family and friends were also with them.

As Ibn Al-Athir has written:

> *These 500 people refused to proceed, and the first man to make an excuse and thus refused to continue walking alongside Ibn Ziyad was Sharik ibn A'war. These 500 people intended to stop moving to*

---

[206] Muhaddith Qumi, *Nafas ul-Mahmum*.

[207] Ibid.

prevent Ibn Ziyad's progress and have Imam Hussain reach Kufa
before he did. Ibn Ziyad, however, kept on going, with a black turban
on his head and a burqa (an enveloping outer garment) on his face,
until he arrived in Kufa.[208]

The people of Kufa, who knew that Hussain (PBUH) was going to join them, were expecting him. When they saw Ubaidullah, they thought he was Hussain ibn Ali (PBUH). Therefore, whenever a group of people passed by him, they would greet him and say, "Welcome, O son of the Prophet of Allah!" Upset by the enthusiastic passion the people had for Imam Hussain (PBUH), Ubaidullah continued his way. At night, accompanied by a group of individuals who had no doubt he was Hussain (PBUH), he arrived at the governor's palace. Nu'man, ibn Bashir, closed the doors of the palace on them.

"Open the door," some of the people accompanying Ibn Ziyad said to Nu'man.

Nu'man, who had assumed Ibn Ziyad was Hussain, said, "For Allah's sake, please get away from here. I swear to Allah that I shall never hand over to you what has been given to me [the position of the governor of Kufa]. On the other hand, I do not intend to fight you, either."

Ubaidullah went over near Nu'man and said, "Open the door if you want to save yourself!"

Someone among the people heard this and said to everyone, "This is the son of Marjanah [i.e., Ubaidullah Ibn Ziyad]." Nu'man opened the door, and Ubaidullah went inside. Then the door was closed again, and the people went away.

In the morning, he had people gather around for prayers. When the people had come together, he took the speaker's position, gave praise to Allah and made his greetings, and then said, "The Commander of the Faithful [Yazid] has assigned me to your district and your taxes. I have been ordered to be fair with the oppressed and give to the needy and the poor. He has commanded that I should be kind to those who obey our orders and treat those who defy our commands severely. I shall obey his orders and carry out his commands among you. For those who do well and those who are obedient, I shall be like a kind father; my sword and my whip, on the other hand, will be for those who disobey my commands and disagree with me. Everyone must be fearful for their lives and try hard to survive."

In his work *Nafas ul-Mahmum*, Muhaddith Qumi has reported that Ibn ul-Sabbaq Maliki has said:

---

[208] As Muhaddith Qumi has quoted in his work *Nafas ul-Mahmum* from Ibn Sabbagh Maliki's *Al-Fusul Ul-Muhimmah*, "When Ibn Ziyad got near Kufa, he entered the city as an unknown, wearing Hijaz attire. He headed toward the city from the desert so that the people would think he was Hussain (PBUH). When he passed by people, they would greet him with respect and say, 'May Allah bless the Holy Prophet's offspring.'"

A group of the residents of Kufa who refused to accept Ibn Ziyad's invitation was immediately killed.

Rumi says:

Whoever pursues wrong, corrupt ways in this world will also incline toward wicked traditions.
On the other hand, good human beings are attracted toward fine customs.
The divide between these two ways has always been deeply rooted among the people,
and will continue to be so until Resurrection as well.[209]

By "salty, poisonous water," lies, oppression, selfishness, greed for power, conflicts with realities and seeing oneself as the end and others as the means are indicated.

On the other hand, "sweet, refreshing water" implies sincerity, honesty, righteousness, the moderation of selfishness, collaboration, and cooperation, establishing correct relations with truths and realities and seeing oneself and others as heading toward the same goal.

---

[209] Rumi's *Mathnawi*, Book 1.

Part 23

Dressed in a Black Turban and an Outfit Common among the People of Hijaz, Ibn Ziyad Arrives in Kufa with a Hussain-like Appearance and Prepares to Murder Imam Hussain (PBUH)!

The Salty, Poisonous Water of Human Life

This is what describes the wicked betrayal that has, in the name of politics, brought the history of mankind – no matter how well-equipped with computers – to halt in the very primitive era. The only difference is that in eras of the past, the man was motivated to achieve evolution and progress due to his hope and enthusiasm, whereas in our times, the astonishing developments in sciences and industries have left no hope in our lives, not even for tomorrow.

In this chapter, we will discuss the black turban-clad Ibn Ziyad's arrival in Kufa in a Hussain-like appearance in order to murder Imam Hussain (PBUH).

It is indeed this very evil that has continued and made a modern man feel futile and aimless. A number of Western and Eastern scientists of the last two centuries believed that advances in knowledge and the development of various kinds of communication (human beings' communication with their own selves, with Allah, with the universe and with their fellow human beings), mankind would gain more power in facing truths and realities and, as a result, there would be no more lies or deceptions. In fact, however, not only did such hopes fade away but as science and industry advanced, lies and deceptions grew to a terrible extent. Consequently, whenever an individual or a group of people rose to a high position of social management, using such ways of wrongdoing (lies and deceptions) became a more legal and deserved approach for them! The even more shameful fact is that the trend of the destruction of human values and the annihilation of the basics of humanity has been given a sacred name – politics! This is the amount of incapability man has shown throughout history.

The Sweet, Refreshing Water of Human Life

Muslim ibn Aqil acted on good human virtues; although he had the chance to kill Ubaydullah ibn Ziyad, he did not do so, as we will see in the following discussion.

Ubaidullah Ibn Ziyad had arranged to pay a visit to Sharik ibn Al-A'war at Hani ibn Urwah's house [during the time Muslim was at Hani's house as well]. "When you hear me ask for water," Sharik told Muslim, "come out and kill Ibn Ziyad."

Ibn Ziyad was sitting beside Sharik, and his servant Mehran was standing nearby. Sharik said, "Give me some water." He repeated his request three times, but Muslim made no move to kill Ibn Ziyad. When Ibn Ziyad had left Hani's house, Muslim came out. "Why did you not kill him?" Sharik asked. "Because of two qualities," Muslim replied, "First, Hani did not want Ibn Ziyad killed in his house. Secondly, the Holy Prophet has been quoted to have said that faith prevents the believers from killing a human being secretly and by surprise." Sharik ibn A'war assumed that the Prophet had meant that no faithful believer was to be killed by surprise and secretly. Thus, he said, "By killing Ibn Ziyad, you would have killed a wrongdoing, corrupted, deceiving, non-believer." As Ibn Nama has been reported to have said:

> "Sharik asked Muslim why he didn't kill Ibn Ziyad. 'When I was going to come out to do so,' Muslim replied, 'a woman in tears approached me and said, 'For Allah's sake, I beg you not to kill Ibn Ziyad in my house.''[210]

It is well known that Muslim refused to kill Ibn Ziyad due to his belief that a man should not be killed in circumstances where he is taken by surprise. In any case, both of the possibilities explored below arise out of the finest of human virtues (in other words, the sweet, refreshing water) which conflict with political deceptions, betrayals, and tricks. There are two possibilities here:

The First Possibility: Hani, the owner of the house, and his wife did not want Ibn Ziyad to be killed in their residence.

The Second Possibility: The murdered man was to be killed in circumstances where he was taken by surprise and had no awareness of what was happening to him (i.e., he was to be assassinated).

It can be stated that if human beings satisfied and continued their individual and social lives based on the dignity of honesty and a realistic approach, even though today's scientific developments and industrial progress would have taken a very long time to be achieved, at least they would have avoided unconscious progress and would not have fallen captive to today's fatalistic machine-like life.

Having heard about Ibn Ziyad's arrival and the intense threats he had made, Muslim left Mukhtar ibn Abi Ubaydah Thaqafi's house for Hani ibn Urwa's house. He asked for Hani, and when he saw Hani, he said, "I have come here to be near you and be your guest [i.e., to seek refuge with you as your guest]." "May Allah bless you," Hani replied, "you have put me into trouble. Had you not entered my house already, and had you not put your trust in me, I would rather have had you leave my house, but ever since you set foot into my house, I am under an obligation. Come in." Hani provided

---

[210] This occurred after Muslim learned about Ubaidullah's visit and his threats.

Muslim with a place to sit. Shiites secretly frequented to Hani's house to see Muslim and advised one another that the whole affair should be kept under wraps.

The humanistic behavior Islam emphasizes can be observed in the conducts of Muslim ibn Aqil, and Hani ibn Urwah and how their behavior conflicts with deceptions carried out in the name of cunning and politics. Hani pointed out that Muslim's entrance into his house had necessitated Hani's providing him with a safe haven. Hani's words – "ever since you set foot in my house, I am under an obligation" – reiterates the age-old human truth that the right to seek refuge is even worth undergoing peril or sacrificing oneself for. The Holy Quran has also pointed out, as seen in the following verse:

"And if anyone of the non-believers seeks your protection then grant him protection ..."[211] that granting refuge is an essential matter. Centuries later, the West also included the rights of those seeking protection in the articles of human rights. In fact, it is governments who are obliged to carry out this law rather than individuals, and if individuals grant refuge, such an action must conflict with what is right for the community. In these circumstances, granting refuge and protection to someone or a group of people is morally appropriate, but not mandatory.

Regarding Hani and Muslim, Hani knew that Yazid's government was a corrupt one [otherwise, he would never want to get himself killed in the atrociously suffering way he did by Ibn Ziyad]. Moreover, Hani's act of providing Muslim with refuge and protection was a great sacrifice which – as Hani himself had also admitted – put him in the danger of being persecuted by the ruthless Ubeuydullah ibn Ziyad, and eventually led to Hani's martyrdom. The Islamic-human conduct Muslim displayed, however, is too obvious to need to be expressed through such ordinary concepts or to be expected to be realized by today's machine-intoxicated people.

There is no so-called social, political or ethical logic in our era which can comprehend the incredible immensity of the law of the prohibition of retaliation before the occurrence of a crime and the prohibition of murdering or assassinating someone in a secret fashion by means of the element of surprise. The roots of such honor, dignity, and greatness in conduct can be observed in the life of Ali (PBUH) and his son Hussain (PBUH).

As historians have reported, whenever Ali (PBUH) saw Ibn Muljam Muradi – the man who would eventually kill him – he would recite the following verse:

> *I want this man to have a life, but he wants me dead;*
> *Tell me what this man's excuse is in this conflict of opposites*
> *...*[212]

Now let us return to Imam Hussain's conduct regarding such supernatural

---

[211] Repentance (9:6).
[212] Ibn Al-Athir, *Al-Kamil fil-Tarikh*, Vol. 3.

issues. On the morning of Ashura, before the battle between good and evil had begun, a man fully armed and equipped for battle quickly approached the tents of Imam Hussain (PBUH) and his men. When he saw fires burning around the tents, the man shouted,

> "O, Hussain! It seems you have rushed toward the flames of this world before you encounter the afterworld!"
> "Who is that?" Imam Hussain (PBUH) asked. "It could be Shimr ibn Thiljawshan."
> "Indeed, it is him," his men replied.
> "O, he whose mother took goats to graze," Imam Hussain said [referring to the decadent, lowly clan Shimr came from], "you are the one who deserves to be in flames."
> Muslim ibn Awsajah then wanted to shoot an arrow at Shimr and kill him, but Imam Hussain (PBUH) did not allow him to do so. "Let me kill him," Muslim told Imam Hussain, "for he is the most despotic tyrant of them all, and Allah has placed him in our range."
> "No, don't," Imam Hussain replied. "I do not want to be the one who started the battle."[213]

From a historical point of view, it is obvious that had Shimr been killed there and then, the bloody story of Karbala would have turned out to be quite different, for it has been shown that Umar ibn Sa'd did not want Hussain's blood on his hands. Historical records show that he even tried to make Ubaidullah ibn Ziyad change his mind about killing Imam Hussain (PBUH).

This is where legal rights, moral ethics and proper aspects of social life come into contrast with one another. On the one hand, since no crime has been committed yet, the law states that no measures should be taken seeking revenge or punishment. Furthermore, abstract moral ethics also agree with the law, condemning any vengeance or punishment prior to the crime happening. On the other hand, when there is certainty about the occurrence of a crime, it would be like the law or any legal right to defend human lives must sit in a corner and witness murders and other crimes, waiting for the murder to take place before it can take any action!

It appears that the prevention of crime, in any way possible, is an essential matter.[214] In other words, when the occurrence of crime is certain, especially in the very near future, all measures must be taken in order to prevent it, for instance by means of arresting the criminal or disabling the means of crime. If the crime cannot be prevented, the rule of disruption needs to be followed. Regarding the rule of disruption, the more important should receive priority over the important. This is a rational, reasonable rule which has been accepted and agreed upon by all legal systems and religions.

---

[213] Muhaddith Qumi, *Nafas ul-Mahmum.*

[214] On the other hand, if there is a long period of time until the crime is to take place, it is natural for there to be the chance that it will not happen.

In regard to Imam Ali and Imam Hussain, however, it can be stated that although the knowledge bestowed upon them due to their positions as Imam allowed them to be aware that they would be killed by certain persons, they did not know what Allah's supreme knowledge had in store for them – as the Holy Quran has stated:

Allah eliminates what He wills or confirms, and with Him is the Mother of the Book.[215]

Therefore, their certainty – which was based on their position as *Imam* and the commander of Muslims – was in no way in any conflict or contrast with the possibility of their killing not occurring even though they were endowed with absolute, endless divine knowledge.

In regard to Muslim ibn Aqil's story, not only was there no absolute source of divinely endowed knowledge, but there was even no normal certainty either, for Muslim reckoned that the people who had pledged allegiance to him would not desert him when it came to battle. Nonetheless, the issue of the prohibition of murder regarding the prohibition of vengeance and retaliation prior to the occurrence of crime calls for serious research, particularly considering the fact that if there is certainty that the crime will occur, there will be no difference between being killed due to the prohibition of retaliation or revenge prior to the crime and being killed when facing the killer in battle. On the other hand, defense – even if it may involve killing the assailant in battle or during any kind of confrontation to kill – has also not been prescribed.

> Shiites frequented Hani's house secretly and cautiously. They also advised one another that these visits must remain completely private. By now, 25,000 people had made a pledge of allegiance with Muslim ibn Aqil. Thus, he decided to begin his war against Ibn Ziyad. However, Hani told him not to act in haste.[216]

Considering the number of warriors who had come to Muslim's aid at the onset of Ibn Ziyad's arrival in Kufa, it seems that Muslim had made the right decision. Now, why did he accept Hani's suggestion? Hani may have known better about how things were in Kufa and Yazid's tyrannical governance. He also knew that such a number of warriors would not stand much of a chance against of victory, either. He was also certain that Muslim's men would gradually grow in number and thus Muslim would eventually have sufficient forces to defeat Ibn Ziyad.

> [A true prodigy of the Machiavellian school of thought,] Ubaidullah Ibn Ziyad called one of his servants, Ma'qal, gave him 3000 dirhams and told him, "Go and find out where Muslim ibn Aqil and his followers are located. Give them this money, and announce that

---

[215] Thunder (13:39).
[216] Shaikh Abbas Qumi (also known as Muhaddith Qumi), *Nafas ul-Mahmum*.

you are on their side. Gather as much information about them as possible."

Ma'qal went to the mosque to see Muslim ibn Awsajah, whom people said asked people to join sides with Muslim ibn Aqil. At that moment, Muslim ibn Awsajah was saying his prayers. When he had finished his prayers, Ma'qal – Ibn Ziyad's spy – told him, "O servant of Allah! I come from Damascus, and Allah has blessed me by granting me the kindness of the Holy Prophet's family. I have three thousand dirhams, and I would like to meet the man from Kufa who represents the Prophet's family and accepts people's pledges of allegiance to the Prophet's offspring. As I have heard, you are informed in such matters, so I have come to you so you would take this money and give it to your master, which will allow me to make my pledge of allegiance to him. If you wish, you can tell him about my request first before I go and see him."

"I am happy to have met you," Muslim ibn Awsajah replied, "for our meeting will give you what you wish for, and through your act, Allah shall also help the family of His Prophet. I cannot bear to see people prevent me from advancing this matter before the means for Imam Hussain's success can be prepared by his representative, for this tyrant [Ibn Ziyad] is a truly appalling creature. "Muslim ibn Awsajah had Ma'qal make serious vows and pledges to keep their agreement to himself and avoid causing any trouble. Ma'qal came to see Muslim ibn Awsajah for several days to persuade him to take him to see Muslim ibn Aqil.[217]

Such acts of espionage and deception aiming to attain people's secrets have been quite a common phenomenon throughout history. The important point which needs to be considered is whether such a phenomenon – which conflicts with principles and laws – should be allowed for any reason or motive (even profiteering, gaining dominance) or should it be only prescribed when it comes to attaining a legally confirmed right. It is obvious that pure consciences and sound common senses of human beings, as well as all divine religions and schools of thought, approve of the second incentive and insist that selfish motives such as acquiring power or seeking profits should be avoided.

Even in those cases which attaining people's secrets and persecuting them can be allowed, should there not be any jurisdictions or conditions set for such a phenomenon which contradicts principles and laws? In other words, if such an unlawful act has been prescribed due to circumstances of urgency, can it be allowed without any conditions? Certainly not. The most important condition which needs to be noted here is that the one who issues the order and also the one who executes it should be highly pious people to avoid any violation of rights during such acts.

---

[217] Ibid.

In this case, the man who issued the order – Ubaidullah Ibn Ziyad – was a true example of tyranny and oppression, a man intoxicated by power and obsessed with violating others' rights who was, in turn, the sacrifice of a live idol – Yazid, the son of Mu'awiyah. The man executing the order, on the other hand, is Ma'qal, an ally of Ibn Ziyad's. Naturally, Ma'qal would set no conditions or jurisdictions in order to execute the order of his wrongdoing master. Furthermore, Maq'al had even made serious pledges and vowed to Muslim ibn Awsajah that he would do nothing to put Muslim in peril and would avoid telling anyone about their agreement. Indeed, this is how a human being can contend his own self as an effort to execute inhuman, anti-Islamic orders given to him, and thus ruin his existence and his being both in this world and in the afterworld.

> *Ma'qal, Ibn Ziyad's servant, and spy, frequently visited Muslim ibn Awsajah after Sharik ibn A'war had died. Then one day Muslim took Ma'qal to see Muslim ibn Aqil and had Ma'qal make his pledge of allegiance to Muslim. Thamamah Seydawi, who was in charge of the treasury and the weapon supply, was also ordered to take Ma'qal's money. A man of wisdom and insight, Seydawi was a renowned Arab warrior and also a distinguished figure among Shiites. Ma'qal continued visiting Muslim ibn Aqil and delivering information to Ibn Ziyad. At this time, Hani had made illness an excuse to cut himself away from Ibn Ziyad's command. Ibn Ziyad asked Muhammad ibn Ash'as, Asma' ibn Kharijah [and also, as reported by some historians] Amr ibn Hajjaj Zubaydi [the father of Ruye'ah Um Yahya, the wife of Hani ibn Urwah] about Hani and why he had cut off contact with Ibn Ziyad. "I have heard that he sits in front of his house, and he seems to be well now," Ibn Ziyad told them, "Tell him this is not a time for him to neglect his duty." The men went to Hani and told him that the governor was asking about him. "He said that he would have come to visit you had he known you were sick, but now he knows that you are well and sit in front of your house. He asked us why you do not go to see him, and you are well aware that no ruler or king will excuse any delay or unsuitable act. For Allah's sake, mount your horse and come with us." Hani did so, but when they approached the palace, Hani felt something evil was awaiting him, and said to Hesan ibn Asma' ibn Kharijah, "My dear nephew, I fear that man." Hesan replied, "I see nothing for you to fear. Allow yourself no excuse to be intimidated or possessed by the governor." He was, however, unaware of what was going on. The men, accompanied by Hani, went to see Ibn Ziyad. Seeing Hani, Ibn Ziyad pointed to him and said, "The traitor's feet have brought him here." When Hani got near Ibn Ziyad, Shuraih Qazi was there as well. Ibn Ziyad recited the verse Imam Ali (PBUH) would chant when he would see Ibn Muljam Muradi: "I want this man's life,*

but he wants to kill me. Tell me what excuse this Muradi man has regarding this contrast."[218]

*   *   *

Until then, Ibn Ziyad had treated Hani with respect. When Hani heard the above-mentioned verses of poetry from Ibn Ziyad, however, he said, "What is going on?"

"I am surprised, Hani!" Ibn Ziyad replied, "What is this wicked conspiracy against Yazid you have started within your house? You gather weapons and warriors to confront him, and you think I would not find out?"

They spoke for quite a while, and then Ibn Ziyad sent for Ma'qal, whom he had sent over to spy out on where Muslim had been hiding. When Hani saw Ma'qal and recognized him, realizing that this man was, in fact, Ibn Ziyad's spy, he remained dazed for a while, and then said, "Hear me out and confirm what I say, for I swear by Allah that I will not lie to you. I did not invite him here, I swear to Allah, and I had no idea what he was doing, either. I saw Muslim ibn Aqil sitting beside my house. He asked to be let in. I did not have the heart to turn him down; I felt that I should bring him into my home and treat him as my guest. If you want, I can leave something here and go and send him out of my house and come back here."

"No," Ubaidullah said, "I swear by Allah that I will not let you leave unless you hand Muslim ibn Aqil over to me."

"I will never bring my guest here for you to kill him," Hani replied.

"I swear by Allah, that is what you have to do."

Hani insisted, "I swear by Allah that I shall never do so."[219]

As Ibn Nama has written:

I swear to Allah that even if I had Muslim ibn Aqil under my foot, I would never raise my foot to allow you to gain control over him. 'For Allah's sake,' Muslim ibn Amr al-Bahili said, pulling Hani aside to give him a word of advice, 'you will get yourself killed. This man Ibn Ziyad is a cousin of the Abi Talib clan. He will never kill Muslim or cause him any harm. Hand Muslim over to Ibn Ziyad. That will mean no disgrace or fault for you, for you are handing this man over to the governor.' 'I swear to Allah,' Hani replied, 'that doing so will be indeed a huge disgrace. I shall not hand over my guest as long as I have a sound body and mighty arms. I swear to Allah that even if I were helpless and crippled, I would not hand him over to Ibn Ziyad, let alone now when I am capable of defending my guest.'

"O philosophers, legal scholars, economists, politicians, literary figures, artists,

---

[218] Ibn Al-Athir's *Al-Kamil fil Tarikh*, Vol. 3.

[219] Ibid.

authorities on psychological fields, analysts of the history of mankind and pioneers of pioneer culture! In the midst of the winding paths the last two centuries have gone through – and have come to be famously known as superhighways of science and freedom, a certain being called "mankind" has been lost! There is no more room for delay. We must rise and attempt to find human beings. In order to do so, we must not forget the pioneers of Allah's enlightening religion and true upholders of moral ethics. We are now in the early fifteenth century Hijra and the twenty-first century A.D. is also just around the corner, and the distance between one who claims "I shall not force a guest who has chosen my house as a refuge to leave my house, for that will put his life in danger, even though such an action may make my own life face peril as well," and another who believes that "I am the end and everyone and everything else is the means!" is, in fact, the distance between humanity and anti-humanity. To see how true this claim is, it would suffice to compare the originality, firmness, and power human life had in the previous eras with the nihilistic, futile human life we witness today."

About the Author

Muhammad Taghi Ja'fari (1923-1998) was born in a religious family in Tabriz, Iran. His parents were pious and greatly respected by the community. The Allameh started formal schooling from the 4th grade, as he had already been taught reading and writing by his mother at home. The Allameh's formal religious education began at the Talebieh seminary in Tabriz, where he became an outstanding student of Ayatollah Shahidi's. He had also studied under the celebrated teachers of his time in Tehran and Qom for a while, but his real mentor advised him to attend the Najaf School of Theology, where he stayed for 11 years. He made remarkable progress and was awarded the highest degree of jurisprudence – *Ijtihad* – at the young age of 23. After completing his education, he began teaching at Najaf.

Ja'fari is a contemporary sage who has expounded his theory about the sociology of Islam. His domain of interest includes practical issues and problems faced by people in their social lives. He is an original and innovative thinker in providing genuine solutions being well versed in Islamic *fiqh*, methods of Western philosophy, and knowledge as it is advanced by social sciences. He has continued the tradition of great masters like Allameh Tabatabaei, the martyr Ayatollah Seyed Muhammad Bagher Sadr, and the martyr Ayatollah Motahhari to bring classical Islamic knowledge in modern diction to quench the thirst of youth with the eternal spring of original knowledge. To realize the mission, the honorable master Allameh Muhammad Taghi Ja'fari has made innovative use of knowledge extracted from modern disciplines like psychology, sociology, anthropology and political science by rationalizing it in the context of classic Muslim Philosophy and ethics as coded in Nahj-al-balaqeh, Rumi's *Masnavi* and other great works.

His voluminous work speaks unconditionally of the rejuvenation of rational thought in Islam. He offers us a broad range of topics and issues related to human needs and basic rights discussed in various paradigms, such as the arts, the humanities, philosophy, aesthetics, literature, mysticism, psychology, and pedagogy. In spite of being a devoted scholar of Muslim philosophy and also a master of *fiqh* (jurisprudence), he did not ignore the invaluable wealth of wisdom replete in Islamic mysticism. The Allameh had fully realized the powerful impact of classical Greek thoughts in the renaissance of the European World. He knew how to dive deep for pearls of wisdom in the works of ancient philosophers such as Socrates, Plato, and Aristotle as well as modern, e.g., Descartes, Leibniz, Hume, Kant, and Hegel. His great appetite for knowledge also relished the taste of world literature such as Balzac, Dostoevsky, Tolstoy, Hugo, and modern-day physicists including Max Planck and Einstein. He says:

> "The true intellectual should always maintain his contact with the vast sea of knowledge in the flow of time, and make use of current logics, known cause-and-effects and their impacts tactfully to make intelligible life in his society a reality. It is mandatory to feel a personal obligation and do one's duty by taking any number of suitable measures to realize one's mission."

His contemporaries remember him as a man who "never rejected anyone; Allameh Ja'fari was a teacher, not a judge!" His passion was to unveil the unknown about the phenomenon of human life. "Life," he believed, "should always be inspired by the original and must follow originality, or it would be merely a burden on man's shoulders." He can be called the philosopher of life, for most of his intellectual pursuits involved knowing about the relationship between man and society. He believed that "Beyond their appearance, all human cultures have a lot in common, and are inseparably associated." He was in search of that unitary element that devises "common human culture" and was able to present it in uniform styles of life that are observed in all societies and cultures: the 'natural' life style and the 'intelligible' one.

Allameh Ja'fari shared a long and intimate friendship with his contemporaries Muhammad Reza Muzaffar, the great philosopher, and Ahmad Amin, the renowned mathematician of Baghdad University and author of the book *At-takamol fil-Islam ("Evolution in Islam")*. The Allameh also had a great taste for modern social sciences and began his research work with open-minded skepticism. Allameh Ja'fari strongly believed in originality and discussion. Those who knew him well and had witnessed his long years of study and research would admit that nothing was more important to him than asking and answering questions He often shifted from one field of science to another in search of answers to questions, and spent most of his time reading books that contained new scientific material and ideas, which provided him with new questions. He said:

> "Questions actually mean that the questioner is saying that he has encountered a dark point on his path toward knowledge, and is eager to overcome it. Thus, passing the bridges and turns of doubt that are the necessity of the phenomenon we call asking, is quite natural. In fact, we can say that on the long road to knowledge, the more bridges and turns we pass with certainty, the better. That means facing many questions."

The Allameh's epistemic geometry comprises of the knowledge of the mind, the revelation of the heart, tradition and modernity, physics and metaphysics, and law and aesthetics. While the first three sources were the main pillars of his thinking, still the expressions of his thoughts were the result of a dialogue among the different basis of this epistemic geometry, which for its up-to-date research and dialogue, made his works novel and attentive to the debates on the issues and problems faced by the "modern human" in the "modern life".

His first book, *The Relationship between Man and the Universe*, shows the enthusiasm of a young scholar in pursuit of knowledge as well as his firm faith and fortitude in the principles of Islam. The Allameh strongly believed that man and the universe have objectives and attainable goals and these goals are far higher than man's material pleasures and worldly desires. He has explained his theories based upon "the four relationships" and "the six questions." His six basic questions are: Who am I? Where have I come from? Where have I come to? Who am I with? Why am I here? And where do I go from here? The Allameh would never leave mankind to drown in his "what there is;" he always called the man to "what there should be." Looking for moral excellence, he seeks his ideal values and behaviors in Imam Ali (PBUH), regarding him as the best proof of the four relationships (1- man-himself, 2-man-God, 3-man-the universe, 4- man-his fellow humans).

A Commentary, Review, and Analysis of Rumi's Masnawi in fifteen volumes and *A Translation and Interpretation of the Nahj-al-balaqeh* in twenty-seven volumes have a distinct place in the Allameh's body of work. Referring to the former, Professor Nasr has noted in the foreword he wrote for "The Structure of Rumi's Mathnawi" written by Professor Safavi (Safavi, S. G., 2006), "It allowed for the tradition of writing commentaries on *Masnawi*, from Mulla Hadi Sabzevari to Allameh Ja'fari, to endure." Moreover, when the Allameh took the challenge of writing commentaries on these two noble texts, one of which is rendered "the Quran in Persian" by Jami and the other is the immortal work of the Master of Masters, Imam Ali (PBUH), both of these texts were considered obsolete in intellectual circles of seminaries as well as universities. Clergies would hesitate to talk about the *Masnawi* in fear of heresy, and writing commentaries on the *Nahj-al-Balagheh* were considered a virtue, not a science. The Scholarship was, and still is seen as footnoting on important books of *fiqh* (jurisprudence). It was in such an environment that the honorable master unveiled the beauty of the *Masnawi*, restoring its worth and esteem in the creative minds of students and scholars.

By comparing Rumi's sublime and amorous assertions with those of French and Russian thinkers and scholars, with whom modern Iranian intellectuals are more familiar, he reintroduced the *Masnawi* to Iranians who were acquainted with the Western thought and culture only. Afterwards, by writing an exegesis on the *Nahj-al-balaqeh*, "A Manifesto on Wisdom, Mysticism, and Politics," he familiarized the younger generation with Islam as a religion which is devoid of superstition, factionalism and backwardness, an Islam based on the appropriation of the mind, revelation, justice and love. We deem the Allameh as the revivalist of the spirit of the *Ummah* by role-playing the vanguard of spiritual assets of Islam, the *Masnawi,* and the *Nahj-al-balaqeh*. Not only will contemporary scholars benefit from this beacon of light, but the future generations will also continue seeking illumination through this valuable resource.

According to Allameh Ja'fari, the spirit of love and creativity of the mind are the two wings that make humans fly towards the absolute truth. The mind and revelation, science and religion, the mind and shari'a (Islamic law) are all compatible and do not contradict one another. Of course, the mind is the solid pillar of knowing (episteme). His political vision renders justice, compassion, mercy, tolerance, serving the people, reliance on consultation (*Shura*) and shared decision-making as the founding pillars of Islamic governance.

Ja'fari was genuinely a humble and modest person, sound in character, and gentle in mannerism. Despite his high stature, he always kept a low profile, neither exaggerating nor exhibiting traces of arrogance and contemptuousness for others. He completely devoted himself to the cultivation of rational thought in Muslims, preparing them to get into intelligible life. The book *Intelligible Life* has been authored on the basis of the ideas that Allameh Ja'fari has dealt with in the 8th volume of his 27-volume translation and interpretation of the *Nahj-al-Balagheh*. These ideas mainly belong to the fifth decade of the Allameh's intellectual life.

He passed away on 15 November, 1998 suffering from a cancer disease. He was buried in Dar-Al-Zohd, by Imam Reza's Holy Shrine in Mashhad.

The Allameh Ja'fari Institute

Index

Index of Concepts

Bibliography

1. The Holy Quran
2. Abduh Al-Shumali, *Dirasat fi Tarikh ul-Arabiyyat ul-Islamiyyah* (originally in Arabic).
3. Abdul Rahim Qanimat, *A History of Great Islamic Universities.*
4. Abdul Razzaq al-Muqarram, *Maqtal al-Hussain.*
5. Abu Bakr ibn al-Arabi, *Al-'Awasim min al-Qawasim* (*"Defense Against Disaster"*).
6. Abu Na'im Al-Isfahani, *Dala'il al-Nubuwwa* (*"The Signs and Proofs of Prophethood"*).
7. Abu Na'im Al-Isfahani, *Hilyat al-Awliya'.*
8. Ahmad ibn *Atham* al-*Kufi, Tarikh Atham Kufi.*
9. Ahmad ibn Hanbal, *Musnad.*
10. Ahmad ibn Abi Yaqub, *Tarikh Yaqubi.*
11. Ahmad ibn Yahya al-Baladhuri, *Ansab ul-Ashraf.*
12. Ahmad Zaki Safwat, *Jamharat Rasa'il ul-Arab.*
13. Al-Alayli, Abdullah, *Sumaw Al-Ma'na Fi Sumuw Ath-That Aw Ashi'ah Min Hayat Al-Hussain* (*"The Loftiness of the Meaning in the Loftiness of the Essence, or Rays from the Life of Hussain"*).
14. Al-Amili, Jafar, *Dirasat wa Buhuth fil Tarikh wal Islam* (originally in Arabic).
15. Al-Aqqad, Abbas Mahmoud (1963): *Al-Hussain: Abu al-Shuhada* (*"Hussain: The Father of Martyrs"*).
16. *Al-Bahrani*, Abdullah Nur-Allah, *Maqtal al-'Awalim.*
17. Al-Bukhari, *Sahih al-Bukhari.*
18. Al-Haithami, *Majma' al-Zawa'id.*
19. Al-Halabi, *Al-Sirat ul-Halabiyah.*
20. *Al-Hindi*, Ala'iddin *Ali* ibn Abd-*al*-Malik Husam*uddin al*-Muttaqi, *Kanz al-Ummal* (*"Treasure of the Doers of Good Deeds"*).
21. Ali ibn Yusuf Qafti, *Tarikh ul-Hukama* (originally in Arabic).
22. Al-Jawzi, *Tathkarat ul-Khawas.*
23. Ali bin Ahmad al-Samhudi, *Wafa al-Wafa bi Akhbar Dar al-Mustafa.*
24. Al-Kulayni, *Usul al-Kafi.*
25. Allamah Tabatabai, *Tafsir-e Al-Mizan.*
26. Al-Mufid, *Kitab al-Irshad* .
27. Al-Sayyid Muhammad al-Alawi al-Hussaini, *Al-Nasa'ih ul-Kafiyah liman Yatawalla Mu'awiyah.*
28. Al-Sayyid Mustapha Al Ul-I'timad, *Lum'at min Balaghat al-Hussain: Khutub, Rasa'il, Mawa'iz,* Karbala, A'la Publications.

29. Al-Suyuti, Jalaliddin, *Al-Jaami' al-Saghir.*
30. Al-Suyuti, Jalaliddin, *Al Khasais-ul-Kubra.*
31. Al-Suyuti, Jalaliddin, *Tarik ul-Khulafa.*
32. Al-Tabarani, *Al-Mu'jam ul-Kabir.*
33. Al-Tabari, Muhammad ibn Jarir, *Tarikh al-Rusul wa al-Muluk* (*"History of the Prophets and Kings"*), often referred to as *Tarikh Al-Tabari.*
34. Al-Zarkali, *Al-A'lam* (*"The Renowned"*).
35. Aram, Ahmad, *Science in Islam* (originally in Persian).
36. Ashtiani, Sayyid Jalaliddin, and Corbin, Henry, *Selected Works from Iranian Divine Philosophers.*
37. Avicenna, *Risalatun fi Daf'il Ghamm min Al-mawt* (*"A Book on How to Avoid the Sadness about Dying"*).
38. Aristotle, *Nicomachean Ethics.*
39. Attar Neishabouri, Farididdin, *Mantiq it-Tair.*
40. Baha'uddin Ali ibn 'Isa al-Irbili, *Kashf al-Ghumma fi Ma'rifat al-A'imma* (*"Lifting the Hardship in Knowing the Leaders"*).
41. Bana, Hassan, *A Political History of Islam.*
42. Bernal, Jon D., *Science in History.*
43. De La Croix Castries, Henri Marie, comte de, *L'islam: impressions et études.*
44. De Lacy O'Leary, *How Greek science passed to the Arabs.*
45. Dinwari, Abu Hanifah Ahmad ibn Dawud, *Al-Akhbar Al-Tiwal* (*"General History"*).
46. Du Pasquier, Claude (1937): *Introduction À la Théorie Génàrale Et la Philosophie du Droit,* Paris.
47. Durant, Will, *The Story of Civilization: The Age of Faith.*
48. Enayat, Hamid, *Political Thoughts of Contemporary Islam.*
49. Ezzati, Abulfazl, *The Political Philosophy of Islam,* (originally in Persian).
50. Fadhlullah, Sayyid Muhammad Hussain, *Al-Islam wa Mantiq ul-Quwwah.*
51. Farhad Mirza, *Qamqam.*
52. Fathi Uthman, *Al-Fikr ul-Islami wat Tatawur* (originally in Arabic).
53. France, Anatole, *The Garden of Epicurus.*
54. Frischler, Kurt (1977): *Imam Hussain and Iran.*
55. Ganji Shafi'i, Muhammad ibn Yusuf, *Kifayat ul-Talib fi Manaqib Ali ibn Abi Talib.*
56. Hamidullah, Dr. Muhammad, *Al-watha'iq us-Siyasiyyah.*
57. Hammerton, John, *A Popular History.*
58. Hunke, Dr. Sigrid, *Allahs Sonne über dem Abendland"* (*"Allah's Sun over the Occident"*).
59. Ibn Abi l-Hadid, *Sharh Nahjul Balaghah.*
60. Ibn Al-Athir, *Al-Kamil fil Tarikh.*
61. Ibn Al-Athir, *Usdul Ghabah Fi Marifat us-Sahabah.*
62. Ibn Al-Ikhwah Damishqi, *Ma'alim ul-Qurbah fi Ahkam ul-Husbah.*

63. Ibn Hajar al-Asqalani, *al-Isaba fi tamyiz al-Sahaba.*
64. Ibn Hajar al-Asqalani, *al-Sawa'iq al-Muhriqah.*
65. Ibn Hajar al-Asqalani, *Tahdhib al-Tahdhib.*
66. Ibn Hisham, *As-Sirat un-Nabawiyyah ("The Biography of the Prophet").*
67. Ibn Kathir, *Al-Bidayah Wan-Nihayah ("The Beginning and the End").*
68. Ibn Khaldun, *Kitāb al-Ibar wa-Diwan al-Mubtada wa-l-Khabar fī Tarikh al-Arab wa-l-Barbar wa-Man Aṣarahum min Dhawi ash-Shan al-Akbar ("Book of Lessons, Record of Beginnings and Events in the History of the Arabs and the Berbers and Their Powerful Contemporaries").*
69. Ibn Khaldun, *Al-Muqaddimah.*
70. Ibn Qawlawayh, *Kamil al-Ziyarat.*
71. Ibn Qutaybah Dinwari, *Al-Imamah wa' Al-Siyasah*
72. Ibn Sabbagh Maliki, *Al-Fusul Ul-Muhimmah.*
73. Ibn Sa'd, *Tabaqat.*
74. Ibn Shu'ba Al-Harrani, *Tuhaf ul-Uqul ("The Masterpieces of the Mind").*
75. Iqbal, Muhammad (1930): *The Reconstruction of Religious Thought in Islam.*
76. Isa Bek, Dr. Ahmad, *Tarikh ul-Bimaristanat fi Islam* (originally in Arabic).
77. Jafari, Muhammad Taqi, *An Interpretation and Critique of Rumi's Mathnawi.*
78. Jafari, Muhammad Taqi, *A Translation and Interpretation of the Nahjulbalaghah.*
79. Jafari, Muhammad Taqi, *Science and Religion in Intelligible Life.*
80. Jafari, Muhammad Taqi, *Universal Human Rights.*
81. Jordaq, George, *Sautu'l Adalati'l Insaniyah ("Ali: The Voice of Human Justice").*
82. Leicester, Henry Marshall, *The Historical Background of Chemistry.*
83. Machiavelli, Niccolo, *Discourses on Livy.*
84. Machiavelli, Niccolo, *The Prince.*
85. Majlisi, Allamah Muhammad Baqir, *Bihar ul-Anwar.*
86. Malik ibn Anas, *The Biography of Umar ibn Abdul Aziz* (originally in Arabic).
87. Masudi, *Muruj-ul Thahab.*
88. Mez, Adam, *Die Renaissance des Islams.*
89. *Mieli, Aldo, La science arabe et son rôle dans l'évolution scientifique mondiale.*
90. Mudarrisi, Allamah Sayyid Muhammad Taqi, *Al-fikr ul-Islami* (originally in Arabic).
91. Mudarrisi, Allamah Sayyid Muhammad Taqi, *Al-Mujtami' ul-Islami* (originally in Arabic).
92. Muhammad al-Alawi, *Al-Nasai'h ul-Kafiyah.*
93. Muhammad ibn Qawlawayh, *Kamil Al Ziyyurul.*
94. Muhammad Khalafullah, *Al-Thaqafat ul-Islamiyyah wa l-Hayat ul-Mu'asirah.*

95. Muhammad Kurd Ali *Al-Islam wal Hadharatul Arabiyyah*, (originally in Arabic).
96. *Muhib al-Tabari, Zakhair ul-Uqba.*
97. Mustafavi, Sayyid Hussain, *Bismarck* (originally published in Persian).
98. Mutahhari, Murtaza, *How Iran and Islam Have Served One Another.*
99. *Nahjulbalaghah.*
100. Najmabadi, Dr. Mahmoud, *A Post-Islam History of Medicine in Iran* (originally in Persian).
101. Nallino, Carlo Alfonso, *Storia dell'astronomia presso gli Arabi nel Medioevo Evo.*
102. Nasr ibn Muzahim, *Waq'at Siffin ("The Battle of Siffin").*
103. *Nasr, Sayyid Hussain, Sources on the History of Islamic Sciences.*
104. Oparin, A.I., *Life, Its Nature, Origin and Evolution.*
105. Paine, Thomas, *Rights of Man*, translated by Dr. Reza Mobasheri.
106. Planck, Max (1932): *Where Is Science Going?*
107. Rashad, Muhammad, *Philosophy Since Earliest History* (originally in Arabic).
108. *Rousseau, Pierre, Histoire de la Science.*
109. Rumi (Jalaluddin Muhammad Balkhi), *Divan-e Shams.*
110. Rumi (Jalaluddin Muhammad Balkhi), *Mathnawi.*
111. Sadr, Sayyid Muhammad Baqir, *Al-Islam Yaqud al-Hayah ("Islam Leads the Life")* (originally in Arabic).
112. Safi, Lutfullah, *Rays of the Greatness of Hussain (PBUH).*
113. Safwan Jammal, *Misbah.*
114. Sahibuzzamani, *Islam's Contribution to the World's Civilization* (originally in Persian).
115. Sarton, George, *A History of Science.*
116. Sarton, George, *Introduction to the History of Science. Volume I, from Homer to Umar Khayyam, and Volume II, from Rabbi Ben Ezra to Roger Bacon.*
117. Sayyid Ali Hamadani, *Mawdah al-Qurba.*
118. Sayyid ibn Tawus, *Luhuf ("Sighs of Sorrow").*
119. Shablanji, Mu'min ibn Hassan, *Nur Ul Absar Fi Manaqib Al Nabi Al Mukhtar.*
120. Shabrawi, *Al-Ittihaf.*
121. Shaikh Abbas Qumi (also known as Muhaddith Qumi), *Nafas ul-Mahmum.*
122. Shaikh Kamaluddin Al-Damiri, *Hayat -ul- Hayawan.*
123. Shaikh Tusi, *Amali.*
124. Shams al-Din Muhammad ibn Mahmud Shahrazuri, *Nuzhat al arwâh wa rawḍat al-afrâh.*
125. Sharif, M.M., *A History of Muslim Philosophy.*
126. Shushtari, Muhammad Taqi, *Qamus al-Rijal.*
127. Shushtari, Nurullah, *Ihqaq ul-Haq.*

128. Stoddard, Theodore Lothrop, *The New World of Islam.*
129. Sulayman Al-Qunduzi, *Yanabi ul-Mawaddah.*
130. Syahpoush, Sayyid Mahmoud, *The Fundamentals of Relations and Correspondences in Islamic Management* (originally in Persian).
131. Thomas, Henry, & Thomas, Dana Lee (1941): *Living Biographies of Great Philosophers.*
132. Toynbee, Arnold J., *A Study of History.*
133. Watt, W. Montgomery, *Islamic Surveys: The Influence of Islam on Medieval Europe.*
134. Yazaju, Kamal, and Qattash Karam, Antoun, *A'lam ul-Falsafat ul-Arabiyyah* (originally in Arabic).
135. Zarrinkoub, Dr. Abdulhussain, *The Portfolio of Islam.*
136. Zaydan, Jurji, *Tarikh al-Tamaddun al-Islami ("History of Islamic Civilization").*

www.ingramcontent.com/pod-product-compliance
Lightning Source LLC
Chambersburg PA
CBHW051619120626
46551CB00014B/1860